## Endorsements for *Into God's Country:*

"*Into God's Country* is a remarkable journey from a complacent faith to one that is battle-tested through adversity and grief. Eric Stogner's story of how God prepared him and his wife Katie for her eventual passing from this life to the next is a story of God's grace and how it truly is possible to find joy even in the shadow of death. Months before she died, Eric was given a ninety-minute vision of heaven. His glimpse of eternity was confirmed by five other people who received either a dream or vision related to Katie's graduation to glory. Eric's story rings true and powerful. If you or a loved one are troubled about dying and where you will spend eternity, you will find this book a tremendous encouragement. It offers a sure hope for an eternal future allowing you to face the unknown darkness of death with faith, hope and even joy for what lies beyond the veil of this life."

*Russ Breault, President, Shroud of Turin Education Project, Inc.*

"I love your book! It is well written, and really speaks to the reader – in a way that it feels like it's from the Holy Spirit at times, and in a way that inspires me to be more open to hearing His voice. I feel like I'm there with the people who are having these experiences."

*Dorothy Bullard, retired*
*Prescott, Arizona*

# Author's Note

It had been almost five years since the first diagnosis. Five years of my wife and I riding the rollercoaster of illness and remission that is typical of the life-altering crisis of cancer. I knew that death loomed. But I had no way of knowing how much longer the journey would last or that it would all be over in less than four months.

I also had no idea that God would explode onto the scene, BOOM.

Everything changed. My world was never again the same.

I had an encounter with God in a new and powerful way through a dream that was like nothing I had ever heard about or experienced.

It radically changed my life, and my wife's last four months. But God didn't stop there. He also burst into the lives of four other adults and a 10-year-old girl – all of whom had dreams or visions from God about the passing of my wife, Katie. They all occurred in the weeks leading up to and immediately after her death. Each of these separate experiences brought powerful messages of comfort. They also revealed incredible images of what happens in the spiritual realm when a Believer in Christ passes from this life to the next.

It sounds astonishing to describe, but we were each shown a portion of my wife's journey *Into God's Country*:

Heaven.

In my dream I was dramatically assured everything was ready for my wife's welcoming into Heaven.

God creatively showed me that He is not an impersonal God. Rather, He cares for us, and is at work in the details of our lives.

You can read the Introduction and find out what my concept of God was like before the dream shattered everything I thought I knew about God. As I experienced my dream, I was sent on an emotional ride that raced from amazement to anger and feeling I'd been kicked in the gut to a place of unimaginable peace and not wanting the dream to end.

In the days and weeks that followed, I was overwhelmed and amazed as I learned of and heard about the dreams and visions others were having about the same events. Though the dreams focused around the very personal details of the passing of my wife, when you stepped back and heard all the dreams told collectively in the order that they occurred, it became clear that they told a very universal and complete picture of God's love and concern about our lives. And showed us what we, as Christians, have been given and have to look forward to. It became clear that this story was much bigger than just a personal story that applied only to my family, but it was THE UNIVERSAL story that applies to all who are members of God's family.

Like everybody else, all Christians will die, but we will also all be raised and live again – forever, in Heaven. This is the essence and bottom line of what it means to be a Christian. We all have souls that live forever and the wondrous stories and promises we have heard about concerning Heaven and how to get there are all marvelously true. This book recounts the words and images we were collectively shown and serves to pull back the veil that obscures this mysterious and often fearful transition on the pathway to Heaven.

I am not so much writing my story, as I am simply relating to you the story God has told and revealed to me and through the events I was honored to experience. Also, remember that I am not only telling what happened to me but I am revealing something of *your* story, as a Believer. My hope for fellow Believers in Christ who read this God-inspired book, is that your Faith and Hope of everlasting life and Salvation will be strengthened and deepened and any fear you may have of death will be obliterated.

If you are not a Believer, my earnest hope is that you will gain an urge to explore the Bible in search of the True living God who unconditionally loves you and has a plan and a hope for your future.

*Eric Stogner*

# Into God's Country

**Dreams and Visions show
a Believer's passage to Heaven**

**Eric Stogner**
**with Jim Dobkins**

Copyright © 2017 by Eric Stogner
Cover design by Marti Dobkins and Elijah Dobkins
Published by UCS PRESS

ISBN 978-0-943247-20-5

First printing, November 2017
Second printing, April 2018

Most of the Bible verses quoted in this book are from the New International Version (NIV) translation.

NOTE: Some names in this book have been changed for reasons of privacy.

Also, out of respect for God the Father, Jesus the Son, and the Holy Spirit, all references to God in any of the Triune God forms, the pronouns are capitalized; i.e., He, Him, so forth.

Contact the publisher via publisher@ucspress.com for discount pricing for large quantity orders.

# Dedication

I dedicate this book, first and foremost to God, who is the real author – because I am not telling you a story I wrote or could have imagined; but rather I am simply recounting all that God did during what can only be described as the most spiritually significant season of my life.

Secondly, I dedicate this book to my family – including first wife, Katie; my children, Matthew and Kristen; and my new wife, Clara. You see, there is even a powerful ending that comes after the story I share with you in this book of how God continued to bless me through others. Somewhat poetically, like Job in the Bible, after a season of trial and loss, my *fortune* was also restored two times over when I remarried and went from having two kids (one Matthew and one Kristen) to having four kids (two Matthews and two Kristens).

Well, OK, Matthew, Matthew, Kristen and Christina. But, you get the idea. God has blessed me with almost double of everything – something I could never have imagined. And they are all a great blessing in my life.

# Acknowledgments

In addition to the people featured in the book who each experienced dreams and visions, I could fill many pages with names of people I would like to acknowledge, because so many played key roles in my life during this season of trial and spiritual growth. But a few true stand-outs include:

Jim Weathers, my friend and mentor who walks so closely with God that he sometimes seems to glow like Moses after an encounter with God. Ann Laramore, a co-worker and spiritually-minded friend whose servant heart is always seeking ways to honor God and help others in their hour of need. She helped me hold it all together throughout the hardest times. Also, Jamie Bosworth, another dear friend, along with the guys who are part of my band of brothers who meet in a real log house to learn about and experience God every Friday morning. I guess Jamie is like Aaron to me – another great leader and trusted friend. I think of him as my best man, for the role he played throughout the journey – he actually served as my best man when I remarried.

Finally, the author John Eldredge, someone whom I consider to be a modern-day C.S. Lewis. He is a great teacher and communicator who walks closely with God and has gifted us with outstanding book after book explaining orthodox Christianity and making it so clear and inviting. God used his works to train me up throughout the cancer journey so I would be equipped for what lay ahead.

# Into God's Country

## Dreams and Visions show a Believer's passage to Heaven

# Eric Stogner
### with Jim Dobkins

## About the Author

### Eric Stogner

Eric is the Manager of Kitchen Design in Design & Construction for Chick-fil-A, Inc. in Atlanta, Georgia, and has worked as an engineer, designer and innovator for over 22 years in the restaurant industry, after serving in the United State Army for four years. He earned his BS in Industrial Engineering at Lehigh University, and his MBA at Auburn University.

Eric values time with his family and enjoys various activities, including water sports, boating and travel. He is a former coach and Boy Scout, and he is actively involved in the Christian community through Church, Bible Study groups, and various leadership roles.

Most of all, Eric pursues an intimate and abiding relationship with the Lord. He has a passion for sharing his dream, and the dreams and visions of others that are revealed in his first book, Into God's Country, in hopes that people will conquer their fear of death, and believe that Heaven is truly a real place and the eternal abode of those who believe in Jesus Christ.

Eric was born in New Brunswick, NJ. He currently resides in Peachtree City, GA with his wife, Clara, and is father to four grown children.

## About the Co-Author

## Jim Dobkins

Into God's Country is Jim Dobkins' 13th book credit as author or co-author. He has also ghostwritten several books. Jim scripted the documentary short Someone Who Cares, which was in Oscar competition. He has co-authored True Crime books, and several Faith-Based books with Russ Miller, including *The Theft of America's Heritage, Darwinian Delusion, 371 Days That Scarred Our Planet,* and *The Submerging Church.*

His first book, *Winnie Ruth Judd: The Trunk Murders*, which he co-authored, was nominated for Crime Book of the Year and was a one-month bestseller in the Doubleday Bargain Book Club. Jim also co-wrote *The Ararat Conspiracy*, and authored his childhood memoirs, *The Peach Tree Limb.*

Jim earned his BA degree from Arizona State University, and is a ScreenwritingU Graduate. He lives with his wife Marti in Arizona. They have a son and a daughter, and seven grandchildren.

# Table of Contents

# Introduction: I have a powerful story to share with you.

I have to say right from the start that, prior to this experience happening to me, if someone else had spoken to me the way I am about to speak to you, well, I would probably have felt uncomfortable and would start to back away.

Really, I mean, it feels like I have been a Christian all my life, but in all those years I had never heard of things like I am about to share. I assure you that they are true and real – more real than the things of this world. I just never was told or shown such things before.

Now I can't stop sharing what the Lord has revealed to me. Let me give to you what He gave to me – a glimpse Into God's Country.

## The reason for this book's title.

Right after I and the other five people had experienced dreams and visions about the process of my wife's passing from this physical life into the next life, all my friends were unanimous that I write a book.

All except one.

That person questioned why I felt I wanted to write a book and share this story with others. I was stunned by this response.

Frustrated by this opposition, I could not stop thinking about it as I left work that afternoon. I became more and more agitated as I drove home, thinking, "Why does he think this story does not need to be told? Is it not obvious? It's stupendous, amazing, and frankly, out of this world."

As I drove, I mindlessly hit the button on my car satellite radio to find a song. I knew that might take my mind off the subject. The title of the song that first came up flashed on the screen:

Reason to believe

I didn't recognize the tune, so I immediately changed the channel. The next title was:

In God's Country

I did a double take and said, "WHAT?"

And began switching the knob back and forth. The readout kept flashing:

Reason to believe – In God's Country
Reason to believe – In God's Country

"YES," I shouted. "That is exactly why I want to write this book! – To give people a reason to believe in God's Country."

And this story is not just a reason to believe in the Kingdom of Heaven. It has so much more. God revealed His heart toward us, how He operates, how He holds the keys of life and death and how He truly never leaves or forsakes us.

He demonstrated what death and resurrection and ascension actually look like in the spiritual realm. He shared what we will look like when we receive our restored bodies. He showed the lengths He will go to reach out to and rescue one more soul.

Truly, the term good news is an understatement. The Gospel is great news – the greatest news ever told. So, those two song titles sum it up:

## Reason to Believe In God's Country

And, even this little story of how those words flashed before my eyes, at precisely the moment I was troubled with a question, a concern of the heart, is an illustration of one of the ways God can work. This was no coincidence and over time I have almost stopped believing in coincidences. So often, they are God-instances. God is a creative and gifted communicator, preferring sometimes to wink or nod gently – like flashing just the right words on a satellite radio display at just the right moment. Yes, He can do that and, yes, He does do that.

The message was clear to me:

WRITE THE BOOK.

This is a story that God meant to be shared. Others also pointed out that if this story was just for me, just to comfort me at a difficult time, my dream by itself would have been sufficient. But the fact that five others had related dreams in the same time period, clearly shows that this is meant for a much larger audience.

God did not act in secret this time – in fact, it seems that He wanted to reveal a lot of His truths to a wide audience.

Most Believers go around with a vague sense of what happens when we die. This true story removes the veil and provides great hope and excitement for what lies ahead and beyond the horizon of this world.

I knew I had to share the hope and the joy, and the reality of what it means to be a Christian, and what we all have come to inherit as a Believer in Jesus Christ.

## The end of the story.

If you have read through the Bible, you know the end of the story:

God wins.

The Evil One loses.

Revelation is a fascinating book. Genesis tells us how everything began. Revelation tells us how everything will end.

While I would never wish the hardship that I experienced on others, I would wish to be able to pass along the deep revelation of truth God gave me in the process.

I thank God that He interrupted my life and the lives of four other adults and a 10-year-old girl with dreams and visions that gave us more reasons to believe in God's Country.

## My former viewpoint of God.

Much of my life I thought God was distant and uninvolved:
An absentee God.

My view of God was one of a benevolent clockmaker. He must be a genius to invent and create the world, with all its intricacies of life. But once created, He wound it up with a key like a clockmaker winds a clock, and then set the world on a shelf and let it run its course, essentially unattended, until the clock spring runs down at the end of the age.

Oh yes, He did spend a season tending to His creation, sending Jesus down to set some things straight and give a more thorough description of the Creator's intents, but after Jesus left, the clock went back on the shelf and we who live on this earth were essentially left to fend for ourselves in this world God created.

God seemed distant and unavailable. I certainly saw no evidence that God was actively involved or at work in the world. Everything seemed to be on auto pilot.

I knew nothing of the Holy Spirit, the third part of the Triune God. But now that has all changed. The story I have to share is not only the powerful climax of how God opened the eyes of my heart to this reality, it goes well beyond that.

To me it is an even more powerful and more universal revelation of also what He does when a believer passes into the Kingdom of Heaven and Into God's Country.

He truly is a caring God who loves us unconditionally. He wants so much for us to live with Him that He keeps giving us opportunity after opportunity to accept eternal salvation through Jesus the Christ. One famous author once referred to God as *the hound of heaven* because He is so intent on pursuing us.

This is already a fantastic truth if you are my Brother or Sister in Christ.

If not, I pray that this book will spur you to open the door to your heart when Jesus knocks on it.

## What this book is. And is not.

This is not a book about cancer, or how to fight and beat cancer.

It is a book about learning to recognize God's presence in your life, including in the good times and in your suffering and troubles. Psalm 34:19 says "the righteous person may have troubles, but the Lord delivers him from them all." I hope to show and confirm that you are never alone. I also want to help everyone I can to see and become aware of the hallmarks of God's love, God's plan and His fingerprints on your life.

This book provides examples of how God uses affliction to seek His children, to draw His sheep to Him, to refine them and bring them into Christ-likeness.

I look forward to hearing from you after you have read this book.

# Prologue: Leading up to my dream

## September 18, 2009

### Early Morning

It felt like I had been jolted with a high voltage shock. My emotions had been turned inside out and upside down.

Yet when the angel spoke I did not want the experience to end.

But right now, my mind reeled. Breath came rapidly like I'd just run a marathon.

I was in my bed. Yet I felt like I'd just been somewhere else and that I had just been dropped back into my bed from a fairly high place.

The clock was right where it should be, on the night stand: 5:30 a.m.

WHAT?

It seemed that I had just stared at the clock, and it was 4:00 a.m.

My mind struggled to reconcile that bit of information: 4:00 o'clock and 5:30 a.m.

Whatever happened to me took an hour-and-a-half. And that was the unmistakable sense of it. Something *happened* to me. Something so powerful and so new that I did not have the words to describe it.

I fell back on the bed, emotionally drained by a strange combination of almost every emotion you can feel happening all at once.

But why?

What had just happened?

I desperately tried to reconstruct and analyze the events of those 90 minutes and remember the contents of my dream. Was it a dream? For a minute there I couldn't even distinguish whether what I had just experienced was a dream or was real. Though I was lying in the comfort and safety of my own bed, there was no doubt that just moments before I was somewhere else. I assumed I must have been dreaming. After all, I was in my own bed. But, then again... No – this was different – very different.

This was so completely over-the-top – so absolutely real, in full color and detail. This was no ordinary dream. Frankly, it didn't feel like a dream at all. It felt extremely real.

The truth is that I rarely have dreams. If I do, I usually wake with no memory of anything going on in any kind of dream – good or bad. The few times I have remembered something, it was usually just a snippet of action; typically me observing some random event from the sidelines with little, if any, coherence or meaning. This dream or vision was entirely different and extremely riveting.

So, without even thinking whether it was even possible, I just closed my eyes and tried to *get back into the dream*. Whatever it was, it was so real and ended so abruptly that I thought somehow I might be able to pass back through whatever portal I had just fallen out of to get back to the action where I was only moments before. I soon discovered that there was no getting back into the dream. Try as I might, I could not simply will myself back there. Instead, I lay on the bed and repeatedly cried out loud as I reached up toward the ceiling:

"Lord, what was that? WHAT WAS THAT? What did You just do to me?"

I somehow knew, without question, that what just happened was from the Lord. There was no other thought or sense of doubt whatsoever. It felt like the Lord Himself, or some other being from the spiritual realm, had just taken me through an experience. As I lay there and started to calm down, the details started flooding back to me.

After sleeping in the same position all night, I remember popping wide awake and glancing at the clock. 4:00 in the morning. I am not a morning person. I never enjoy waking up early and rarely wake up alert and refreshed. Yet for some reason on that morning, I just popped wide awake at 4 a.m. for no purpose I could determine.

There was another reason that the idea of waking up well-rested was such a distant memory for me.

It had been about four-and-a-half years since my wife, Katie, had first been diagnosed with breast cancer. Though she had a remission period for a while, it had been about a year since the cancer reoccurred in other parts of her body – bones, liver, and lymph nodes.

As with anyone whose wife is fighting cancer, I shared in Katie's battle fatigue every waking and sleeping moment. No matter where I went or what day it was, I also faced the stress and disappointments of the cancer struggle that was causing her life to ebb away.

This particular morning, however, I had awakened at 4:00 and felt very rested. Ninety minutes later I was an emotional wreck, recalling a very detailed series of events that seemed to be just moments old. At 4:00, when I was awake, I remembered thinking, "Even though I am awake and rested, I don't really feel like doing anything else at this hour." I was not struck with the idea of getting up, reading, spending time in the Word, or anything else, so I decided to try to roll over and go back to sleep. Even this was unusual. I have always had a hard time getting back to sleep after being awakened, especially since being in the midst of fighting cancer. Oddly, this time I was able to drift back to sleep very easily.

In fact, in retrospect, it almost seemed like I was *put to sleep*. Who knows? All I know is that when I closed my eyes it was 4:00 a.m. and now it was 5:30 a.m. During that time something seriously rocked my world. I was still trying to grasp what I just experienced.

What also was different – rather than the dream being fuzzy or fragmented, this multi-sensual experience came back in precise detail. I not only remembered the plot, but all kinds of details about the setting. As I recalled the dream, I could feel the atmosphere of the rooms, hear the noises and dialogue, and see the elaborate details of the rooms I was taken through. As I replayed the dream, there was a sense that, if you were watching it on a video it would only take about ten minutes in all to watch, and yet it also had felt timeless, as if time had been suspended.

At the time of the dream, life felt uneasy, but stable. There was an expectation that Katie's health could gradually worsen, but also a hope and desire that any decline would be delayed and perhaps she could live with the cancer for a long time. Both my parents survived for over a decade after their cancer reappeared. Katie and I hoped for a similar long run before things got worse.

Little did we know what was coming, or what the Lord was about to say and do in our lives. Of course, God knew, and it was in His perfect timing that the following events unfolded in our lives.

... and noticed what appeared to be an angelic being standing near the door on the other side of the room. The being stood out in stark contrast from the surroundings, but I sensed only I could see him or her. Mari and Jack did not seem to be aware of this stranger in the room.

It felt odd, not scary, but definitely out of the ordinary that some tall being was standing there in the room watching us. I really could not tell if the being was male or female. A strong sense of strength and vitality emanated from this being. I tried to look at its face, but could not see it – or was not permitted to look upon it. It was whited out, glowing like the sun.

An angel in light.

# Chapter One: My Dream

As the dream opened, I could immediately sense that I was very tired, standing alone in a bedroom next to a queen-size bed. I looked down at the bed and, because I felt so tired, I just flopped forward down onto it – thinking a short nap would do me some good.

But, as I lay there, my mind began piecing together what was happening around me and perhaps why I was so tired.

It felt to me as if my family and I had reached a destination – as if I had just finished driving my family – wife, Katie; son, Matthew; and daughter, Kristen – in our minivan on a very long trip to some sort of family reunion.

It felt similar to trips we'd made when driving from Georgia to visit relatives in New Jersey for the holidays. But this trip felt like it had taken even longer – perhaps three days – due to inclement weather or something.

Typically when we traveled in those days, Katie read and the kids watched videos while I drove.

This trip felt more difficult than any others, as if I had been concentrating on the road for a long time, my knuckles white from gripping the steering wheel while navigating through snow and ice.

As soon as we arrived and entered the house, the cumulative weariness overwhelmed me, and I looked for a bedroom to take a nap.

Though sleepy and lying face-down, I took notice of the bed-spread. It was white with a large, textured circular pattern in the fabric. White fringe surrounded the edges and hung down near the floor.

I noticed that my heart was weary in a different way from my body. Although I felt a sense of merriment at some occasion, there also was a heaviness and sense of dread about this visit.

Off in the distance I heard what sounded like a small crowd of relatives gathering in another room, saying their hellos, catching up with each other:

"Oh my, look how much you have grown."

"You have not aged a bit…"

And on and on.

I thought I recognized the voices of close relatives, including Katie's parents, her siblings and their families. I wanted to join them, but on the other hand, I wanted to rest for a while and catch up with them a little later.

As I lay there, I wondered what specific holiday we might be there to celebrate. Again, there was this sense of joy and excitement to see others at this special time, but I also had the sense that we were gathering because of Katie's declining health – as if the time to spend with her was limited and precious.

At this last thought I started to feel bad about avoiding the group, and decided I really should get up and join the others. But before I could get up, I heard someone calling out my name like he was looking for me. The voice got louder. It was a child, my nephew, Jack. He came around the bed, approaching my head, and kept repeating, "Uncle Eric? Where are you?" in that sort of child-like *sing-song* voice.

Then Jack's mom, Mari (Katie's sister), came in the room and sat down on the bed behind me. I felt the bed move. I had been found, hiding from the crowd and trying to rest.

"Oh well," I thought, "so much for a quick nap. I guess there is no rest for the weary."

Though disappointed that I could not rest longer, I was truly glad they found me. I rolled over to take a look at them, and as I did, I looked up into Mari's face. Our eyes locked and we smiled at each other. It was a happy greeting, but we also shared a *knowing look*. I could tell she also felt a sense of mixed emotion: gladness to see one another, but sadness because of the context of the gathering.

Regardless of why we had come, it was clear to both of us that there was a sense of urgency in the air that we all needed to be together around Katie.

## An Angel in Light

Turning my gaze from Mari toward Jack, I saw beyond Mari, over her shoulder, and noticed what appeared to be an angelic being standing near the door on the other side of the room. The being stood out in stark contrast from the surroundings, but I sensed that only I could see him or her. Mari and Jack did not seem to be aware of this stranger in the room.

It felt odd, not scary, but definitely out of the ordinary that some tall being was standing there in the room watching us. I really could not tell if the being was male or female. A strong sense of strength and vitality emanated from this being. I tried to look at its face, but could not see it – or was not permitted to look upon it. It was whited out, glowing like the sun.

An angel in light.

The brightness of the angel's face blotted out every facial detail.

The angel beckoned me with an arm motion to get out of bed. As soon as I began to move, I suddenly no longer felt tired at all. I just sat up and arose with little or no effort.

Although I don't know whether this angelic being was male or female, I will assume – for the sake of telling my dream – the angel was female.

She seemed to be urging me to follow her out of the room. As we neared the door, I could hear and sense that all the others were in a nearby room off to the right, still greeting each other with excitement and anticipation.

But, instead of turning right and heading toward the sound of the voices, the woman turned left. Not a word was spoken between us as I followed her down a short hallway.

We stopped at the end of the hallway and paused just inside a doorway. After a while she gestured toward the room, as if to say, "Behold!" (Though I don't remember any actual words being spoken.) She seemed to be showing off this room to me, calling my attention to the care and preparation that had been taken by someone to prepare for an important gathering.

The medium-sized room was arranged for a meal or gathering of some sort. I somehow could tell, or better yet, I was *made to know* that the furniture that normally would have occupied the room had all been pushed to the edge of the room to allow for four special round tables. Each table was arranged with eight to ten chairs and dinner place settings complete with dishes, silverware, cloth napkins, and a centerpiece.

It seemed the room was made up this way in preparation for a large gathering of people for a meal. There was a sense that a fairly large crowd would be present at this event that would be spread out here and elsewhere throughout the house. I was impressed at how a simple room could be transformed into such an elegant dining area. It looked very well done.

I still was wondering what the actual occasion was, and who all the guests were to be.

The woman then began walking forward through the room. I followed her as she moved gracefully between and around the tables, heading toward another doorway on the opposite side of the room. Once again, she stopped in the doorway and gestured into the next room that was beyond this doorway as if to say, "Behold!"

## In a heavenly place

This time, I was startled as I looked into the second room because of the nearly-blinding bright light that flooded this second room. I had to blink and squint my eyes to adjust to this bright light.

I could see that two of the four walls – the wall to my left and the wall straight across from me – were made entirely of glass and looked out to a green, lush yard. Or at least there were green shrubs and grass just outside the windows. The sun or illumination outside was very bright.

I remember wondering where I was and thinking that perhaps if I could look outside through these glass walls, I would recognize the landscape and get a clue as to where we were. So I raised my eyes and began to look outside. But the sky was filled so much with light that I could not see any blue sky at all – just bright light.

Outside was nearly a total white-out. It was exceedingly bright, but not painful, though I did have to adjust my eyes and was unable to look out the window for more than a few moments. All I could see were the shrubs and grass immediately outside the windows. As I looked further away, all was blotted out with blinding light. In fact, what it did look like was what you see when you are in an airplane climbing up through a cloud just before breaking through the top. The windows are filled with white but you can't see any features or anything in the distance. It occurred to me that I was in no ordinary place. Looking for familiar land-marks out the window was futile – I was in a place that I had never been before and it felt like a heavenly place. Not that I really knew what Heaven might be like, but it was just a sense of it – like a place suspended in the clouds up in the heavens. I have never felt or sensed this before or since.

In order to regain my sight, I directed my eyes back inside the room. All the while, the woman just stood silently nearby, gesturing again around the room, as if beckoning me to take a closer look at everything. Again, she seemed to be calling my attention to all of the detail and care that had gone into the preparations.

Indeed, this room was spectacular and even larger and more beautiful than the previous room. Like the first room, I was made to understand that the existing furniture had been pushed out of the way to the corners of the room to make room for another four to six tables and chairs in the middle. This room had the same kind of round tables and chairs with white tablecloths and white chairs, but the table settings were even fancier than those in the previous room. On these tables were formal china, stemware, fancy table decorations, and centerpieces. There were large glass vases in the center of each table with brightly colored flowers. Strings of white pearls and strings of silver beads were placed in a zig-zag pattern around the vases on each table.

Along one wall there were decorative palm trees made of wicker and painted bright white. These palm trees were also decorated with the same kind of white pearl strings and silver bead strings draped from branch to branch. It was quite glamorous without being overdone.

I remember looking down at a place setting and noticing that this time there was not just one plate at each seat, but multiple plates and multiple pieces of silverware. There were three or four pieces of stemware per place setting. I was stunned by the level of detail and care that had been put into each place setting.

Though I am typically not one who cares much about decorations or enjoys formal dinners, I was very impressed and amazed at how well it looked. There was a real splendor to the room. I knew that this was going to be an amazing event – one to be remembered long and well.

Finally, after taking in every detail of this second room, the woman turned to her right and began to move through this room toward another doorway in the wall to the right. I followed her as she led me past the tables. This time, rather than pause at the doorway, we walked all the way into a third room.

This room, the largest of the three, was by far the most beautiful and formal room of all, with columns of ornate woodwork. The southern-style windows ran nearly floor to ceiling, and, though they were decorated with fine drapes, they allowed just the right amount of that bright, outdoor light to enter and fill the room so that the space was very pleasantly illuminated. This seemed to be the room where the main event would occur. It had a grand entrance foyer that connected it back to the rest of the house.

Standing in the middle of the room, I stood by her side. This time the woman did not have to gesture or invite me to behold the room.

## A place prepared

I was surrounded by splendor I had never experienced and needed no invitation to look around. The entire room exuded elegance and formal flare. We were standing near the middle of the long room. The theme of the rooms was starting to become apparent to me. I was seeing a place prepared – well prepared.

On one end of the room there was an open grand piano, revealing the strings within. Next to the piano was a tall silver candelabra with many candles burning brightly. On the opposite end of the room was a massive fireplace with a large ornate mantle. On the mantle were two more large candelabras also holding many candles that were lit. The room was filled with fine china and expensive-looking objects displayed around the perimeter of the room. The floor was covered with brightly-colored oriental rugs, and there were fine linens elegantly displayed.

Everywhere I looked I saw white and silver, including the table, chairs, china, and place settings. As in the previous two rooms, I could see that the couches and other furniture that belonged in the room had again been either pushed to the side or temporarily removed to make room for more round tables and chairs. The place settings were even more spectacular than those in the previous room. These were plates of the finest china, sterling silver flatware, crystal wine glasses and pitchers. The centerpieces were made up of ornate crystal vases filled with colorful fresh-cut flowers. White linen napkins were set in silver napkin rings. This room was fit for a king and was made up to perfection.

I sensed that the house was to be filled with many guests of family and friends. I could still hear in the background that the others were in a room not too far away, still excitedly greeting each other. However, as I looked in the direction of their voices, I could not see any of them, though I could see a few other rooms between where we stood and where they were. These also were well decorated and in full formal splendor.

There was this sense that the entire place was very clean, bright, and exquisitely prepared for a special event. I could tell that absolutely nothing else needed to be done; no last-minute cleaning or preparation or anything to worry about. It was perfect, like no place I'd ever known.

All was well and would be ready for the remaining guests and visitors to arrive shortly. All the while, as I took all of this in, the woman in white was standing next to me. She had still not spoken a word, but her presence permeated the room.

Then, for whatever reason, my gaze was drawn down toward the floor. Something near the leg of one of the chairs caught my attention. It was an old grey-and-black, 1960's vintage movie camera – the kind that used old super 8 movie film – sitting on the floor by the table closest to me. I immediately knew whose it was and why it was sitting there. This was my father's camera that he had used to film our family when I was a preschooler in the late 1960's. I realized that this was probably a head table, and was where my father was to sit at this celebration. I understood, without explicitly being told, that my father must have set his camera there to be able to film the upcoming event. This was just like my father, always ready with the camera to capture the moment.

The thought occurred to me that I had arrived at this event in my family minivan. As is my custom, I often bring a video camera to capture events. I felt certain that I had packed my camera. I figured I surely could take much better videos of this event with my modern digital video camera than what my father would be able to capture using that old relic from the 1960's. I was ready to race out to my car, get my video camera, plug it in to be sure the batteries would be fully charged, and have it all ready for this event. I turned to leave the room and get my camera. Even though I still did not know where I was, I did, at least, still have a sense of where my car was parked, relative to this room.

This is where the dream really gets interesting.

I had nearly forgotten about the woman in the room who had led me there in the first place and showed me all this splendor. As I started to step away, she seemed to reach out and touch my arm as if to stop me from leaving the room so quickly.

I remember thinking, "Oh yeah, you're still here."

She was standing next to me and still had not actually spoken a word. I did sense, however, that I was in close communication with her and that she was somehow sending me thoughts and making me understand things. She exuded this strange sense of calm and serenity. I sensed that she was to my left and had reached out and touched my left arm. When she did, I froze, almost shoulder-to-shoulder with her.

## The voice

She broke her silence. She spoke in what I can only describe as an *other-worldly* voice. It sounded incredibly beautiful, like a mixture, somehow, of speech and music – beautiful symphony music. It was like every word I heard spoken from her lips had a harmonic background sound track. I remember thinking, "Wow! Can you just keep talking? Just say anything – the alphabet, non-sense words, anything. Keep talking so I can hear more of that incredible sound."

And before I reveal what was spoken to me and the dramatic rollercoaster of emotions it was about to send me on, I want to pause and camp out here just a moment longer. You see – I am unable to say enough words or the right words to fully share with you just what the sound of this heavenly voice was like. It was beyond words to describe. I can only describe it as deeply harmonic and sublime. Imagine that you are standing on the 50-yard line of a massive indoor football stadium and the stands around you filled with people. Only these people are all members of a world-renowned choir and they are all singing in perfect 12-part harmony, all at once. The stadium is filled with perfectly-tuned and harmonic music. The ground seems to resonate, as does your own bones, with the sound of the music – and you are in the middle of it all. That is what just the sound of the voice felt like to me.

Her words were both powerfully calming and reassuring.

This is what she said to me, in the most matter-of-fact kind of way you could imagine:

**"You know, she is leaving us soon."**

Immediately, I knew, or was made to know, exactly who she was referring to and what it meant. I knew with complete certainty that *she meant that Katie would be passing away soon.*

I was stunned; instantly filled with feelings of great pain, angst, concern, anger, fear, and defensiveness. I felt like I had just had all the wind taken out of my body, and that in its place, deep angst had risen up inside me.

It was as if every negative emotion, every hurt, every pain, every frustration and every disappointment that had been collecting over time concerning the battle against the cancer and the pending loss of my wife were suddenly welling up like a huge black tsunami-sized tidal wave on a sea of emotional unrest. It hit me so suddenly and so forcefully that I reacted to it like reeling from a gut-wrenching blow.

I stepped forward one pace and pivoted to my left to fully face this messenger. I wanted to confront this woman who was so harsh as to say such a thing. As I spun around, I was so angry and hurt that I almost wanted to punch her. Instead, I just thrust out my hand toward her in an angst-filled gesture. I can still clearly picture my arm extending out toward her, fingers half-clenched into a fist, and reeling with pain and anger. As I turned toward her, and thrust out my hand, I yelled at her in disbelief with all the anger I had inside me, **"What! I'm losing her?!"**

As I tried to look directly into her face, demanding an answer to my question, I noticed that I still could not look upon her face. I could clearly see a white robe, but I could not really see or recognize a face. It remained so radiant and filled with light that I could almost not even look in that direction.

Then, immediately, without hesitation, and without any anger, angst, or frustration in her voice, she replied using that same overwhelmingly beautiful voice of calm serenity, and shaking her head, **"No, you are not losing her. You can never lose her. But, she is leaving you soon."**

Again, I froze. All I could do was stand there like a statue for a moment, stuck in that stance as I had gestured toward her. I can still remember seeing my arm extending out from me and my hand in a half-fist of twisted pain.

## He calmed the storm.

The reason I think I was stunned, frozen and unable to move was that as those words were spoken, something else was happening to me – inside of me. It was as if radical surgery was *done to me* in an instant, as if some source of intense pain at the center of my being had just been instantly removed and cured. That is why I was standing there stunned. Something powerful had just been done to me, the likes of which I had never experienced before.

That tidal wave of negative emotion, including feelings of anger, fear, loss, frustration, had all just disappeared in an instant and at the first sound of that voice – totally. Finally gone! Not even an echo remained. It was as if that tsunami-sized wave had just immediately fallen down and collapsed, leaving the sea flat, calm and motionless. I had no more emotional turmoil or upheaval. It was all calm and peaceful like the ocean at sunset.

That is what it felt like inside during this *conversation* with the woman in white. I believe it was more of a message from beyond, than a conversation. In any case, when the conversation started, my emotional or internal state felt more or less calm with perhaps a few dancing thoughts or emotions darting about like small spouts or ripples in the emotional pool of my soul. As she spoke the first words, the waters in my heart seemed to become even more calm and at rest, like a pond with not one ripple.

However, as soon as I heard those upsetting words that I perceived meant that I would be *losing* Katie, there arose an amazing swell of internal emotion of angst, anger, and fear all wound together. It felt like a massive column of water rising straight out of the center of my soul, filled with all the fear, hurt, pain, and misery that this cancer experience contained. Yet, as soon as the second set of words were spoken by the woman in white, the massive column of water just collapsed immediately and was absorbed without so much as a splash or ripple in the water. All was calm and tranquil again, perhaps even more tranquil than before. With no explanation, and in the blink of an eye, all the negative emotions that had welled up inside me simply melted away, disappearing beneath a tranquil sea. I later reasoned that this is what it must mean when scripture says God can *wipe away every tear.*

As all this was happening, I was not made to forget the pain of any of my troubles or my past. If anything, I was able to remember and perceive them in more detail than ever. Nevertheless, at the sound of the angel's voice, those painful thoughts and memories simply had no more pain attached to them. There was no fear, no angst.

It was amazing.

As I took all this in and absorbed all that was happening to and around me, I remained motionless. Then I felt the sense that I was about to fall forward and was off-balance, since I was still standing there, leaning forward with my arm still thrust out in front of me. So, it was not out of fear of the angel, but simply to avoid falling down, that I took one step backward, away from her.

As I straightened up and relaxed my arm, I remember thinking over and over again, "Who are you? Who are you that you can say those things and do those things to me?"

I kept wanting to know her identity and to see the face of the one who had done this to me, so I started looking this woman up and down once more and tried again to look at her face.

While attempting to focus on her more clearly, I noticed that the field of my vision seemed to immediately expand and enlarge. I had not realized it up to that point, but it had been as if I had been seeing everything through a pair of binoculars. It was as if I had been fitted with a set of blinders, like a horse sometimes wears, that prevents him from seeing to the side, only allowing him to look forward at what is ahead. I had this sense that my field of view had been somehow limited and I could only look straight ahead. Even though I had been able to look around, I had to move my head in order to do so, to focus on what I was looking at and what I was being shown in greater detail.

As I stood back a pace from the woman, it was as if the blinders fell away and I was able to regain my full peripheral vision. When that happened, I was instantly able to see where I was standing and knew intuitively exactly where I was. I was shocked to discover that it seemed like I was standing in my old childhood house in New Jersey. This flooded my mind. At that moment, in the room where the conversation had occurred, we were standing in the formal living room of my old house.

The previous room (the second room) that was filled with light was our old glassed-in porch, and the first room the woman took me to was our old TV room or den. Even the bedroom I was in when the dream began was my parents' old bedroom, complete down to the actual bedspread with the same annoying pattern on the fabric. It was annoying because it had all these tufts of thread in a circular pattern and if you were to fall asleep on it you would wake up with a polka-dot pattern on your face. This is a minor detail to be sure, but I find it interesting that I noticed and made a linkage down to this and many other very small details.

But, while the house was suddenly very familiar, it was also at the same time very different from my house growing up. What was mainly different was the fact that the house I was now seeing in the dream was much bigger, brighter, cleaner and nicer than our real house had ever been. It was immaculate, like a mansion pictured in a magazine. What also was different from the past was that these rooms were all filled with tables, chairs, and fancy china. It was clear that the entire house was decked out for a major party.

I can tell you that this was no simple memory from my past, because our house never looked this nice, and we had never had any occasion where we rented additional tables and chairs to fill every room. This house looked like a similar version of the house I grew up in, except that it may have been built and occupied by royalty or someone very wealthy like the Biltmore family.

I turned and focused my attention back on the woman – the angel in light. I wanted to hear that voice again and ask her questions. I tried to look at her one more time, but I was still being blinded by the radiance that was emanating from her head.

Then, without actually thinking about what I did next, I simply remember hearing my voice speaking as I asked this woman or angel, "Is that you, Mom?"

I am not sure what possessed me to say that. I do not think I had even fully put together the question in my mind – it just came out. Perhaps I had some vague sense that my mother was involved in this because the room felt like it could be my mother's house. Another reason I may have made this connection was that, in real life, my mother had died a year earlier, and there was a specific sense that she was going to be one of the guests since my father was to be there for certain because I had seen his old camera, and he was still alive. It was totally bizarre, but there was a sudden feeling that this woman standing in white in front of me could possibly be my mother.

As I attempted to look more closely into her face to try to make out any features and continued to ask, "Who ARE you?" I was abruptly blinded by white light. My whole field of vision faded to white, and I felt myself falling back down into my bed in real life. I awoke from the dream.

I sensed that God had arranged or allowed the brief visit or encounter. That He knew that a vision like this would be sufficient to communicate a whole lot to me. That, in His infinite goodness and mercy, He found just the right combination of events to convey a message that would give me a sense of serenity and communicate a very difficult thing to me in a way that I would be comforted and not overwhelmed with fear.

Again, it was so ... of God.

# Chapter Two: What Does It Mean?

As I stumbled out of bed at 5:30 a.m., shaking and even crying, my tears were from a combination of sorrow and joy:

Sorrow over knowing Katie was indeed about to physically die.

Joy in knowing that some sort of joyous reception was awaiting her in God's Country – Heaven.

But so much had transpired – physically and mentally – in my dream that I did not yet fully grasp the meaning. I felt a strange joy and happiness despite being overwhelmed by it all. Yes, my dream was over, but the message from God was not quite complete.

I eventually got up and started my daily routine of preparing to go to work and getting the kids up for school, even though I was a walking wreck and tears were still streaming down my face. Trying to hide my emotions and state of being, I first went into the bedrooms of both my kids to wake them up and get them started for school. I wondered what they might be thinking and how strange I must have looked to them, coming in so early and in that strange state.

Next, I took a shower. That morning, the shower helped wash away my stream of tears and I thought, if you are going to cry I guess the shower is a good place to do it. I remember thinking that I was very glad it was a Friday morning, and I would be going to my men's fellowship, the Log House men's group, where I knew I would be able to tell a few of my closest Christian friends about what had just happened to me.

Surely they could help me make more sense of all that had just occurred. It was all just so much to handle. The dream was packed with so many messages and meanings of peace and comfort, in spite of hearing the difficult news about Katie *leaving soon.*

Whether it was an angel, or the Holy Spirit Himself, this messenger in my dream, and the setting in which it occurred, was successful in showing me the true heart and inner beauty of whomever was responsible for arranging and decorating for this special occasion. It was clear that it was an act of love and service that had created such a welcoming and honoring event. It was also clear that it was not only to honor Katie, but to honor me and other family members as well. It felt like a gift of love, hospitality, and grace to me from the Holy Spirit that came, interestingly, on my actual birthday, September 18th.

I had this strange sensation that felt like a combination of foreboding and yet comfort about the news I had been given. I had a strange sense of detached calm and serenity surrounding the whole thing. As if I needed to be told, "All is well. She will be leaving you all soon, but just for a while, and you will be reunited with her soon."

The pangs of loss and grief I felt were quickly and strangely replaced with a quiet, calm sense of serenity. Yet, in spite of the sense of comfort, I still wept for a long while. I continued crying in the shower while trying to talk with God to find out more about what I just experienced.

"What was that?"

I kept asking the same question over and over, "What was that? What did You just do to me?"

Then a strange sensation overwhelmed me – like I was standing on Holy Ground, surrounded and filled by the Spirit's presence. Even in the shower, it felt like the hairs on the back of my neck stood up and that I was not alone, even in this small, confined shower stall.

I did my best to calm down and stop crying so I could receive more answers. I remembered learning from author and speaker John Eldredge to start praying and using simple *yes* or *no* questions when you want to hear from God. I began by asking simple questions about what had just happened.

"Lord, today is my birthday, was that about my birthday?" (pause)

"No, it wasn't about your birthday," I sensed God's still, small voice say.

"OK." I was just checking. I did not think so either. Maybe it was a holiday, like the sort of event we would have traveled to be with relatives.

"Lord, was that Christmas, because I did not see anything red or green or get much of a sense of that occasion?"

I heard nothing.

So then, I thought, "I know, Lord, it was about Thanksgiving, wasn't it?"

Clearly there was family gathering, and I thought Thanksgiving was a good guess. After all, obviously the rooms were made up for a big meal and there was going to be a lot of fancy fixings served for a crowd. Again, I felt no confirmation in the Spirit that it was set at Thanksgiving, though that interpretation felt closer.

As I thought more about the dream, I sensed that the occasion was much larger and more formal than that.

Then I sensed the Spirit say to my spirit, "No, it is none of those things. It is a wedding rehearsal dinner."

With that, immediately I got a sense that the manifest presence of the Spirit had departed. The hairs on the back of my neck laid back down and I felt like I was alone again in the shower stall. I sensed that that was all I was going to get for now.

As I stepped out of the shower and was toweling off, I thought and wondered about what I had heard. I was a bit stunned and confused at the idea. Wedding rehearsal dinner was just not making sense to me; Thanksgiving perhaps, but wedding rehearsal dinner? But, on the other hand, that is exactly what it felt like in the dream. Suddenly, it all came together with great clarity. Yes, the house was decorated in a very formal manner, not unlike what a wedding rehearsal dinner might look like. In fact, a wedding rehearsal dinner was exactly what it felt like. I could not have put words to it previously, but that was precisely the sense of it.

In the dream, I never sensed that I was seeing or hearing from God or Jesus directly. I could not make out who the being was – an angel perhaps, but not God Himself. I was never told who the person in radiant white was. The being never answered my question or revealed who she or he was. In fact, it felt almost as if I was asking too many questions and that the *curtain* was pulled back down because it would be revealing too much to me – more than I could bear or was ready to hear.

I sensed that God had arranged or allowed the brief visit or encounter. That He knew that a vision like this would be sufficient to communicate a whole lot to me. That, in His infinite goodness and mercy, He found just the right combination of events to convey a message that would give me a sense of serenity and communicate a very difficult thing to me in a way that I would be comforted and not overwhelmed with fear.

Again, it was so ... of God.

## A little help from my friends

I was relieved it was a Friday. Because an hour later, I attended my men's group that met on Friday mornings at a nearby Log House. Through another couple of rounds of tears, I told my dream story to a handful of dear friends, men of faith who were much *deeper* than I was.

By the time I got to the end, including telling the part in the shower up to the last word about the wedding rehearsal dinner, they each said, "Well, of course!"

I thought, "Of course, what?"

They proceeded to explain the obvious meaning of it all that was not so obvious to me at the time.

The dream really did seem just like a wedding rehearsal dinner – the kind of personal event held for close family and friends only.

My friends pointed out that the Bible describes a number of references to a wedding feast. Christ Himself says, in Matthew 26:29, "I tell you, I will not drink from this fruit of the vine from now on until that day when I drink it new with you in my Father's kingdom."

He was making reference to Revelation 19:9 – [9] Then the angel said to me, "Write this: Blessed are those who are invited to the wedding supper of the Lamb!" And he added, "These are the true words of God."

Apparently, there will be a celebration and merry-making on the order of a wedding, and Christ will be raising a toast or sharing a glass of wine. In Matthew 22:2, Jesus said, "The Kingdom of Heaven is like a king who prepared a wedding banquet for his son."

The members of the Church (true Believers in Jesus) are referred to as the Bride of Christ, and Christ is the bridegroom.

It was all starting to make sense. Katie really was going to *leave soon* and be taken up in conjunction with a great banquet, an honor reserved for those who are part of the Bride of Christ.

Wow!

It was all so much to absorb. Yes, this is something we had been taught in our faith, but I never had it spelled out, nor had I experienced the venue of anything remotely similar to a lavish rehearsal dinner as I had just experienced.

There was a sense that *It* was not the wedding. That was to be for tomorrow. Such an event would be in an even larger venue – like a huge hotel or cathedral-like building. No, this was one last event with the bride before she would be united with her bridegroom.

I sense this is what passing into Heaven might be like – the Bride of Christ (His disciples) ascending to be with the bridegroom to a great celebration and to a place prepared for us in advance.

My close friends in the Log House group knew what was happening in my life. My wife had been diagnosed with breast cancer about four-and-one-half years before this dream.

The first year of that journey was hard. At 39 years old she underwent a double mastectomy and a full course of chemotherapy followed by reconstruction surgery. It was difficult for her and the whole family.

Katie lost all her hair and experienced such a difficult roller-coaster of physical, emotional and mental trauma. Thankfully, years two and three were comparatively uneventful times of healing and recovery – or so we hoped. We made every effort to return to a regular life, hopeful that we had *beaten cancer* and she would be a cancer survivor.

Then at the three-and-one-half-year point, some new symptoms occurred. The cancer was back as stage four metastatic breast cancer that had spread into her bones, liver, ovary, and beyond. The treatment plan this time took on a different focus. It was no longer about eradicating and beating the cancer, but was now mostly aimed at slowing the spread and advancement of the disease while maintaining quality of life.

For the year leading up to the dream in September 2009, the disease was kept mostly in remission through the use of hormone suppressive drugs. Though the disease was moving very slowly, our lives were certainly on edge as we lived in a new reality: a world where the cancer probably would not *be beaten* and we were on constant alert for any signs of its continuing advancement.

During the previous months of 2009, we had many new challenges, but she was able to do most of the things in life she wanted to do. To the casual observer, she still seemed quite well. As mid-September approached, there was no observable change in her condition, and we simply lived our lives day-by-day, trying to cherish each day in relatively good health while enjoying life and each other to the fullest extent possible.

I will share with you in another chapter two special prayers that Katie and I prayed that were answered.

Oh, one last thing that seems like an important detail. I remember that as I showered and was reflecting on all that had happened, something else very interesting happened. In my head there was even a soundtrack that seemed to play in the background and rise from within me. It was not something I made a conscious effort to do or think about – I just found myself spontaneously singing – or at least trying to sing – as I wept. Without my own conscious effort, I found myself singing along with an old hymn that I knew from my past that seemed to be playing inside my mind and filled my spirit. It was pure, uninhibited singing of joy from my heart and soul to the Lord. It reminded me of that passage in scripture where the Pharisees try to ask Jesus to rebuke His followers to stop praising Him. He responded in Luke 19:40, "I tell you," He replied, "if they keep quiet, the stones will cry out."

I felt like one of those stones, spontaneously breaking out in song.

The soundtrack was the old hymn *Praise my Soul the King of Heaven*, and in my head at the time I could hear it being sung by an angelic-sounding boy-choir, not unlike the boy-choir I myself had been in when I was in my youth.

The deep and profound words of grace and mercy contained in that hymn so accurately describe our heavenly Father and the feelings I felt welling up from inside me. In that moment, the lyrics felt so deeply true, comforting, and real. Perhaps this is a bit of an example of how we will worship in our hearts continuously when we are fully in the presence of the Lord in the Kingdom of Heaven.

I could not help but sing. Later when I drove to work, I listened again and sang along to this soundtrack in my head (and eventually I found it on my IPOD), praising God and marveling that God would reveal all this to me. It was so deep, so meaningful, so personal, and so comforting. It seems that it can only be from God.

These are the words from that Hymn and the song in my heart:

Praise My Soul The King Of Heaven

Praise, my soul, the King of Heaven,
To His feet thy tribute bring;
Ransomed, healed, restored, forgiven,
Evermore His praise we sing
Alleluia! Alleluia!
Praise the everlasting King.

Praise Him for His grace and favour
To our fathers in distress;
Praise Him still the same as ever,

Slow to chide, and swift to bless:
Alleluia! Alleluia!
Glorious in His faithfulness.

Father-like, He tends and spares us,
Well our feeble frame He knows;
In His hands He gently bears us,
Rescues us from all our foes:
Alleluia! Alleluia!
Widely as His mercy flows.

Angels, help us to adore Him;
Ye behold Him face to face;
Sun and moon, bow down before Him,
Dwellers all in time and space:
Alleluia! Alleluia!
Praise with us the God of grace.

I have told my dream hundreds of times, and it still seems as fresh to me as the morning dew. Every detail of that dream experience was seared into my mind and my soul and has become the most intense personal and spiritual experience of my life. I don't think I can ever forget it – something powerful was communicated; something powerful was done to me and within me.

She was in Jesus' arms – just happily, joyfully, dancing around. It was so beautiful. I felt an overwhelming sense of peace. The image was very calming and filled me with joy.

# Chapter Three: Their Dreams And Visions

The very powerful dream experience I was given provided a huge dose of peace and strength. It opened my eyes to how God can work, and raised a great deal of other questions in my mind and heart.

If that dream was the only time or the only way that God would have spoken or intervened, it alone would have been sufficient for me. It dealt with 80-90% of my emotional grief – washing it away almost completely, and it gave me a deep sense of peace.

But God did not stop there.

He kept going and going, revealing more and more to others, who would begin to come forward and share their dreams with me. What was interesting is that I did not know or did not know well the other people, or only was connected through another person. None were existing or close friends, per se.

Rather than spread these other dreams and visions out along with lots of supporting detail, my co-author and I have decided to give you these dreams up front, one after the other, in rapid-fire succession. So buckle-up, because we are about to pick up the pace and you are in for a wild ride – as I was in real life. It could change your understanding of life and death and God and Heaven forever.

## Dancing with Jesus

Janeen Jamison did not know me or Katie when she was asked to pray for us. Janeen describes her connection to me this way:

I met Jim Weathers at a tea shop called Tea Fusions in Peachtree City (Georgia). On Sunday evenings after they were closed, people were welcome to come together as a community to pray for each other, the community, our country or anyone who needed prayer.

Jim would come to our Sunday night sessions sometimes with his wife Marianne. We became good friends and Jim and Marianne are like family to me and my kids.

Jim called one morning after he had attended the Log Cabin Friday morning men's group that Eric Stogner also attended. He said Eric's wife Katie was in the hospital again fighting cancer and was in serious need of some prayer warriors to help with their situation. Even though I had never met Eric or Katie, Jim had mentioned their situation before at our Sunday night prayer group. I told him, of course I would pray for Eric and Katie. It would be an honor to be one of their prayer warriors.

Several times throughout the day I prayed for them, and also before I went to sleep that evening.

I had a dream so vivid that it still seems like I just had that dream the other day, and not over seven years ago.

In the dream, I saw Jesus and He was dancing with a woman who had shoulder-length, light-brown hair. I didn't see her face. She was facing Jesus. He was taller than her and He was looking at her and smiling and talking to her. Like you would expect of two people dancing. They were both in flowing, white gowns and there was bright light all around them. I didn't hear music or their voices; it was more like I was observing them from a distance.

She was in Jesus' arms – just happily, joyfully, dancing around. It was so beautiful.

I felt an overwhelming sense of peace. The image was very calming and filled me with joy.

Later the following day, I recalled I was supposed to be praying for someone's healing and I just had a dream of a woman dancing with Jesus. If that was Katie dancing with Jesus then she wasn't being healed of her cancer.

I called Jim Weathers to tell him about my dream. We were used to praying for people and hearing they were healed – not that they were going to Heaven. I was a bit shaken by the experience. But Jim was thrilled to hear of my dream and asked me to call Eric and tell him about it. Jim had already heard of Eric's dream so he knew my dream was another piece to the puzzle Eric was trying to piece together.

I was a bit nervous about calling Eric since I didn't know him or Katie, and I wasn't sure how he would take the news of my dream. Turned out, Eric was very interested to hear my dream and has shared it with others. Later, I met Eric in person shortly after our phone conversation so he could hear the dream again. I was even able to visit Katie at Hospice before her passing.

Eric and Katie managed to touch so many lives through their journey. I feel truly blessed and honored to be a small part of the story.

The image of Jesus dancing brings me peace to this day. I certainly don't fear dying when I know I'll be dancing with Jesus in Heaven one day, too.

*Janeen Jamison*

## Eric's Observation

Janeen's dream is a simple but powerful one that focuses on God's love for his children; His immense joy that exudes from Him and affects those around Him.

I picture an outdoor setting like on the beautiful green grass at Augusta National, home of the Masters Golf Tournament in Georgia. A place of peace and perfection. Not a blade of grass out of place. Not one weed. Not one bare spot. Grass soft enough to dance on barefoot.

Notice the intimacy between Jesus and His blessed one. He gets close and shares His Joy. And it is a one-on-one, very personal focus, not like some graduation ceremony where you and 500 other classmates all stand and are recognized. You get to dance with the King! Alone, the center of His attention. Your true place as the apple of your Father's eye is experienced at such a moment. Note also the overwhelming emotion – happiness, unending happiness and joy.

Also, notice the condition of the recently departed – they are fully alive, restored and beautiful. Regardless of the age and condition of the person at the time of death, when they are resurrected, they are at the peak of health and beauty. We get our bodies back, but not the worn-out or injured bodies that we had on earth, but the bodies that God had initially designed for us to have when He knitted us together in our mothers' wombs. These new bodies are heavenly bodies, no longer subject to death and decay, or any other worldly ailments we all have to contend with in this life. Just imagine that.

Finally, notice the clothing – this is significant. Notice both Jesus and His beloved bride are both clothed in flowing white robes. Scripture talks about this a lot – the wedding clothes and the need for clothes that are not stained by sin but are washed and made white as snow. We caught a glimpse of this through this dream and vision. We are given clothes of white, similar to the clothes Jesus Himself wears. This is clothing appropriate for a bride at a wedding and is why even to this day in our fallen world, we know that a bride should be wearing white and it is a symbol of cleanliness and purity. No matter how dark our sins and stained our earthly clothing is, Believers are forgiven of their sins, and their clothes and appearance before God and to others is made pure and white – not a spot of blemish anywhere. All the bleach in the world can't remove the stains of our sins, but the forgiveness of the Father can and does. We will be splendidly clothed in the Kingdom, dressed appropriately to see and be seen by the King Himself.

This is a simple picture that was a confirmation that Katie, indeed, already had a place prepared for her in Heaven. She would be leaving soon for a place where the grass is green. It gave me an incredible sense of peace and seemed to fit with the dream I had also been given.

## Prayer Warriors And Visions

Angela and Jackie Dukes were faithful prayer warriors. They heard about Katie from Jackie's husband Jake, who worked on the staff of the church Katie and I attended.

Their efforts in lifting Katie up to the Lord were so intertwined that they had several visions each, often while praying together. By Jackie's account, "We had multiple visions of Katie's wonderful transition from a frail, dying woman to a joyful, perfectly healthy woman in Heaven."

Here is their story, told in a back-and-fourth conversation between Jackie and Angela:

Jackie:
The visions started the weekend before Thanksgiving in 2009. I was driving in my car, and felt impressed to pray for Katie. Immediately I saw an angel standing by Katie's bed ... and Katie was coming back from the dead. I was thinking, "She's not even dead yet."

There was a long lull. Around December first or second, we – Angela and I – during a Christmas party got together to pray for Katie. As we started praying I saw Katie lying in a coffin. I reached down and could feel her hand. Angela didn't know what I was seeing.

Angela:
I saw Katie in the coffin and in the spirit, I kept saying, "Arise...Arise...Arise..." at the same time Jackie was seeing Katie and grabbing her hand.

And this was at a Christmas party. I've learned that no matter what you are doing or how busy you think you are, when you feel prompting of the Holy Spirit, you respond.

Jackie:
Right up to the week Katie graduated to Heaven, we asked, "Lord, are you asking us to pray that Katie be healed and come back to earth?" OR – as Angela and I began to sense, God was

establishing grounds for endless love. We knew without any doubt that the Lord was showing us a glimpse of a wonderful eternity with Jesus.

Angela:

The day before Katie died, I saw Katie was about to eat an apple ... and the apple was an apple of death. And I was asking the Lord, "Is this of you?" Then I heard the words, "She is going where the grass is greener."

And I saw her walking barefoot on lush grass surrounded by a large garden, with a gentle breeze blowing. It was very beautiful.

Jackie:

I saw her put the apple down. She wasn't able to see what we saw – that the apple had worms in it.

Angela:

I saw a glass of lemonade handed to Katie. I knew it was a glass of new life. It was something specific the Lord had concocted. We handed it to her. "See what the Lord has for you." She drank it down.

In a vision later that day I saw Jackie and me putting all these healing ingredients in this big cup, and Katie's drinking it. After she drank it all, she even put her hand in the cup and wiped the residue on her face, and she wiped it on her arms then across her chest. She laid down, and she said, "If it's Your will then heal me."

Jackie:

Then I saw the hospital bed start elevating to a vertical position ... and she disappeared. A huge teddy bear fell down where she had just been.

Angela:

That night – her last night as a woman of little more than skin and bones – I saw a banquet. Katie had a white princess dress on. Everywhere she started walking, there was this white light ... and then she was on a horse ... and there was water around ... the horse went down into the water. She walked into this room. There were bodies around. It looked like she was walking into a tomb.

Jackie was saying, "Where is she? Where is she?"

Then Jackie's voice got real soft. "Rise up. Rise up."

Jackie:

On Friday, the day after Katie died, I prayed to the Lord, "We need to know about Katie."

I saw Jesus pour lemonade in Katie's mouth. I could see the lemonade as it went down into her body.

Angela:

At that same time I was having a crazy day at work. One of those times when I felt I did not have time, but I felt the prompting of the Holy Spirit. I went to as quiet a spot as I could. In my spirit, I saw a birthday cake. It was a celebration of Katie's life.

The next thing I saw was a grim reaper. He was chopping into Katie's stomach. And then Skittles just flooded out. It was just like ... out of her body. Of all things seeing Skittles coming out of her body. I knew what the Lord wanted me to do. "OK, Lord, I'm going to tell Eric."

I saw Jackie and Katie rolling around on the floor, laughing, talking about what just happened.

Later Eric told Jackie and me that Katie had always liked M&M's. That she never ate Skittles; that is, never except during the last two weeks of her life. She ate nearly all of two large family-size bags of Skittles during that time. It was the only thing she ate in her final days.

Jackie:

While Angela was having those visions, I saw Katie outside the funeral home dancing around in circles – around and around...

Then later that day I saw angels bringing Katie down from Heaven. There was lemonade. She was lying down ... and as

Angela and I prayed for her, she stood up and said, "Where am I? Where am I?"

Jesus came down and He sat in a circle with Katie, Angela, and me. Katie kept saying, "I'm so cold. I'm so cold."

She looked like a frail, old woman.

Jesus gave her some hot tea. Every time she drank some of the hot tea, she kept looking younger and healthier and more vital until finally she looked like she was young again, and healthy and beautiful, and looked to be in her early 20's.

It was a joyous celebration.

*Angela and Jackie*

## Eric's Observation

There was a lot there to comment upon. First of all, what a beautifully-repeated confirmation that Katie was about to be perfectly healed in an eternal way and joyously welcomed to Heaven.

The imagery and meaning here is quite stunning and powerful.

Angela observed angels surrounding the bed of one who is dying – showing the fact that God watches over us and is aware of even a small sparrow that falls, how much more He is aware of the passing of one of His children. He has angels surrounding them at this important time.

She also notes that this is a time of death and that all of us, Believers and non-Believers, will undergo death. Whomever originated this quote, hit the nail on the head:

"The statistics on death are impressive – everyone eventually succumbs to it."

This is a foundational truth – we are not immortal in this life, but for a Believer that is the once and only death; from there we are resurrected and live on in eternity forever. The non-Believers suffer a second death, one that is indeed fearful, for it is the death unto hell – one that is also unending.

Jackie senses God's love – His process of establishing and grounding each of us in His endless love. This is another amazing and eternal truth. Believers are rooted and established in God's love.

The apple represents death – like the apple that is often associated with what Adam and Eve eat in the Garden of Eden. It is a fruit that the Lord implores them not to eat and it is often referred to as an apple that looks good to eat. But it represents death. In her vision, again Katie is eating an apple of death and apparently is not aware that it is filled with worms. Death is a reality in our fallen world and is a metaphor of the original sin that leads to death that we are all born into. Man is born and destined to die, unless he comes to a saving grace that only Jesus can provide. Man's body will suffer a physical death, but his Spirit does not. Death is an interesting milestone – also because often something must first die before it brings forth new life. We all must die a physical death in order to bring about a spiritual re-birth unto new and unending life.

It is also neat how Jackie and Angela again both described Heaven as a place where the grass is greener. They are also shown a glimpse of God's Country where, apparently, there are lush flowers, perfect grass, and gentle breezes. Doesn't the 23rd Psalm that is often read at funerals, describe this in the first three verses? "The LORD is my shepherd, I lack nothing. He makes me lie down in green pastures, He leads me beside quiet waters…"

Doesn't this image that was revealed match that description well?

Then there is the image of lemonade – mentioned in two separate visions. Lemonade seems quite appropriate – don't you think? Lemonade is perhaps one of the most thirst-quenching drinks, especially to someone who is parched. Scripture says in Matthew, 5:6, "Blessed are those who hunger and thirst for righteousness – because they will be filled and satisfied."

Or what about the woman at the well, who is drawing water out, parched in the heat of the day? The Lord told her in John 4:13-14, [13] … "Everyone who drinks this water will be thirsty again, [14] but whoever drinks the water I give them will never thirst. Indeed, the water I give them will become in them a spring of

water welling up to eternal life." What a powerful picture –
Believers are revived by such a refreshing taste of living water,
represented in this vision by lemonade. When we feel dry to the
bones, is there anything more refreshing than a cold glass of
lemonade? Elsewhere in scripture, restoration of a people is
described as bringing life back to dried bones or bringing green
growth into a parched desert.

Notice also, there was a teddy bear – remember that for later,
because for some reason, a teddy bear shows up another time. I
suppose the teddy bear represents comfort. I will also share this –
that neither Angela nor Jackie knew. Someone had given her a
huge teddy bear. It was light brown. It has been a family keepsake
that my daughter Kristen has kept since then. The teddy bear is
one of those huge bears like you might see at a carnival. I don't
remember who gave it to her, but it was in Katie's room and is
with us still today.

Then there is another reference to a banquet and a white
princess dress. Is that not exactly like a wedding dress? The bride
often looks like a princess. This again, is how the Lord clothes His
new bride and how He treats her when she is welcomed into His
Kingdom. There is a lavish celebration and Angela also saw a
birthday cake. Again, how appropriate. We all have cakes with
candles to celebrate each year the birth of our children, honoring
another year of the person's life. How similar the celebration in
Heaven apparently is – there is a birthday cake to top all birthday
cakes with the specific purpose to honor the life of the newly-
arrived saint and child of God.

Then there is another reference to death – like the apple. I
believe the trek underwater riding a horse represents death, or
drowning or descending to the underworld of the dead. It is from
that dark place that they envision rescuing Katie from the dead,
commanding her to arise.

Also, there is a third reference to death – this imagery was
very clear and powerful. Angela actually saw a grim reaper figure
– an obvious image of death and actually saw that reaper chopping

into and savaging the earthly body of Katie. Clearly it shows that she is dying or about to undergo death.

It is comforting that at least she appeared dead already and there were not images of pain and suffering. This is a verification that an earthly body is subject to death.

Finally, there was a tiny, almost insignificant and seemingly odd detail that Angela just mentioned in passing without realizing the impact of it for me. She was made to see in her vision that when death chopped open her body that skittles candy came pouring out. When she told me this she seemed to throw in that detail and move immediately on to the next image she saw. But that detail really struck me as intriguing.

Why?

Because first of all it is odd, and second of all, if a dead person's stomach were opened up, surely something like sugar candy would be unrecognizable – yet she was so sure and specific as to say she saw skittles. Don't you think that is odd? I will now tell you the rest of the story. Unbeknownst to her, Katie never liked skittles, though she had always liked M&M candies. Except in her final days in hospice where she had very little strength or appetite. But, someone had brought a family-sized bag of skittles and left them in the room – probably for our kids. Anyhow, oddly, Katie ate a lot of them, most of the bag. In fact, I would say that perhaps the only thing she ate in the final day or two may have been those skittles. So, when this vision described her being chopped open and skittles falling out, it was as if God were sending ME a very specific detail, that only I would have known as a way of confirming the validity of all of their testimony. Because, frankly, all this was starting to sound a bit over the top – even to me who had fairly recently become a believer in such things. This was, no doubt, a wink and a nod from God – and He was telling me, the skeptical engineer type, that this was all very real.

After those brief reinforcements in the dreams that, indeed, Katie was going to go through death, the Lord immediately revealed more images of restoration and new life. The mention of healing lemonade again, and this time healing tea, administered by the Lord Jesus Himself becomes another powerful image of healing and restoration.

In Jackie's vision, she actually observes the transformation process as Katie drinks the healing liquid, the restoring water that begins to well up inside her and essentially reverses the aging process. In short order she transforms from a frail, fragile old lady who is cold and near dead to a very much alive and vibrant young woman who is rolling on the floor, laughing and again, joyfully dancing with the Lord. Notice even the temperatures mentioned – cold associated with death and the warmth of the healing tea associated with life. Remember even that temperature reference – because that comes up again. Things that are dead are often cold and stony, but things that are alive are warm and vibrant with life.

Just pause and let all that sink in. Reread it all if you like. Think about that for yourself and any loved ones you have that are near death or that have already passed. Let the reality of these deep mysteries flow over you and soak deep into your soul. This is what you are heir to. This is what the Christian scriptures have been talking about. This is what you will experience also if you are a Believer and child of God. This is His heart toward you and all His children. This is the essence of the Christian story – a love story between God the Creator and Father and His beloved children and bride. Nothing can get better than this.

Finally, there was the absolute confirmation after her passing from this life Into God's Country, that she had a perfectly-healthy body. No more pain. No more sorrow. Just abundant life with the Lord forever. Isn't this what we all long for in the deepest part of our hearts – for ourselves and for our loved ones? That is what was revealed. It is all true.

## 10-year-old girl's encounter with an angel

Katie loved children and loved to serve as a teacher or care-giver. And they loved her. Here is the account by Amanda, one of those children she had taught in Sunday School, recording what happened to her soon after Katie's passing from this life into Heaven.

Just a few days before the loss of beloved Mrs. Katie Stogner, I went to visit her in hospice (January 9, 2010. She died five days later.) The last words she said to me were, "I will watch over you, Amanda, I promise. Don't worry about me."

AN AUTHOR NOTE: I'm interrupting for a moment to give you some background. I remember hearing about this visit – though I wasn't there at the time. Amanda came in with her mom and when the two of them entered the room, Amanda took one look at Katie, who by this time didn't look good – all skin and bones, jaundiced. This was a big change from the last time little 10-year-old Amanda had seen her, and Amanda was so shocked and repulsed that she ran from the room. Her mom or other friends went after her to comfort her and eventually they reassured her and were able to get her to come back in the room with her mother to visit with Katie. At this time, Katie was quite weak and did not talk much, but apparently she mustered up the strength to say a few words of comfort to a startled and fearful little girl.

Back to Amanda's recounting of events:

On Thursday, January 14, 2010, the same day Mrs. Katie left us, there is proof that she kept that promise to (watch over) me.

That evening, as I was getting ready for bed, I was lying on the floor of my room on my back, staring up at the ceiling, very upset. It was dark in my room, almost pitch black. I was awake because I had just entered through the door.

As I looked up at the ceiling, an angel appeared. I couldn't make out the face until she was fully formed. Once I did see her face, it was Mrs. Stogner!

She was in a white robe so long I couldn't see her feet. She had the most beautiful face in the universe. And she had the same beautiful smile, and the same sparkling eyes.

It was the most magnificent thing I'd ever seen. I couldn't believe my eyes.

Was this a dream?

What was I supposed to do?

I stared, speechless, at the angel speaking soft words in Mrs. Katie's voice.

She said to me, "Do not be afraid. Heaven is wonderful. I can't wait to see you here someday."

She was healthy and happy.

She loved Heaven.

It was so comforting and exciting.

Then she reached down her hand and I reached up mine.

I felt her firm grasp. Her grasp was very weak (a few days ago) in hospice (but now it was firm and strong).

She was really there!

She held my hand and rubbed her thumb up and down (my hand) as she did to me in hospice. She did this for quite some time, until she slowly faded away without saying another word.

I was too speechless to say anything.

Just then my mom came in to check on me. I was staring up at the ceiling, still too speechless to say anything.

She asked me, "What are you staring at?"

I told her, "Mrs. Katie was just in my room!"

I explained exactly what she said, how she looked, and how she felt.

The next morning, sitting on my dresser, placed ever so carefully so I could see it when I woke up, was a stuffed animal bear. It was white with sparkling angel wings, and it was on his knees praying.

In its hand it held a small glass bottle with a transparent purple liquid that smelled very sweet.

I had never seen this bear angel before in my life.

It was the amazing proof that Mrs. Katie kept her promise.

Just the next day, after Mrs. Stogner came to me, I told Mr. Eric Stogner. He thought that was truly amazing, just as I did.

This was truly an amazing experience that I will remember for the rest of my life. I am blessed to have known her.

*Amanda*

## Eric's Observation

I think it is significant that this is the testimony of a young child. This is an innocent person who would have no preconceived notions and would accept what she saw at face value. What Amanda sees and experiences was while she was alone and awake and was a very personal encounter. And hers, more than anyone else's, shows the power of a comforting spirit. The Holy Spirit is often called the comforter and my dream also gave a sense of deep comfort. It seems as if God is closest to the broken hearted and when things are really tearing us up, vexing us at the soul level, God may send a messenger to provide just the comfort we need to keep going. In this case, to actually see and TOUCH Katie was very powerful.

Notice the similarities – a being that appears first in light and notice the clothing again – a long white robe. But the most striking thing is the wonderful description of her restored body. Amanda kept saying how beautiful she was with sparkling eyes. She even described her as magnificent. How amazing our new bodies will be – they will be so magnificent that we might not recognize ourselves in a mirror, yet others will recognize us. This is how our Heavenly Father sees us and designed us. We will finally look our best – for eternity, and not have to work out or watch what we eat to keep that awesome body. Also, our body will be different as well, apparently able to materialize and dematerialize, probably not unlike the way Jesus, after His resurrection was able to appear and disappear, to disguise Himself and then reveal Himself.

Another powerful thing that I noted when I interviewed Amanda and recorded her testimony on video, was that they actually touched hands. She felt her hand! And she seemed to really gain a lot by that touch. After video-taping her story, I asked her more about that, asking her what it felt like. In childlike simplicity she said something so simple and yet so profound. She said, she felt warm and firm and not like she was in hospice.

Then I remembered that encounter I had heard about in hospice when Amanda ran out of the room, but later was encouraged and coaxed back into the room. The two of them had held hands, so Amanda had gotten a very tactile feeling of what a nearly dead person's hand felt like – probably cool and all skin and bones. The difference a few days later was very striking to her and to me. Katie was healed and felt very much alive. Notice the imagery and use of temperature. The dead feel cold but the alive feel warm and flowing full of life.

I imagine this is how Jesus looked and felt to the disciples when they shared that last breakfast of fish on the shore after Jesus appeared to them after His crucifixion. I imagine Jesus was again trying to get them to grasp, just as Amanda needed to grasp, that those who are resurrected are very much alive. They can be seen and touched and, apparently, can share a meal and eat fish. Katie and Amanda shared a meaningful touch that conveyed a powerful message – the dead are truly healed and raised alive again.

Finally, there is another teddy bear. I don't know much about this bear and haven't seen it myself. Amanda still has it. She and her mom describe it very vividly – a bear left that is praying with angel wings and sweet smelling oil in a container. What a powerful residual message of comfort to a child – a soft bear that prays and smells so sweet.

It was the day after Katie passed that Amanda's mom called me and told me that her daughter had had some sort of encounter but she was hesitant to come over and share it with me and hesitant about how it might make my daughter Kristen feel. By this time, I had already heard the testimonies of everyone else, so I told her to come over quickly and share whatever she had. This too was a powerful source of comfort and it was also comforting to Kristen and Matthew.

God used a 10-year-old girl for absolute confirmation that Katie already was in Heaven. What magnificent grace that God showed by using a girl loved by Katie to show His eternal love for His child, Katie.

I was reminded about what Jesus told Paul on that road to Damascus:

My grace is sufficient.

**The TV was turned off in a one-point game in the fourth-quarter of the 2010 Super Bowl so we could talk about these amazing dreams.**

Brent Merritt and his wife Mary were recent members of the Sunday School class of which I had been a leader. Katie had passed away already on January 14, 2010. Super Bowl Sunday that year was on February 7 – the 24th day after Katie's passing. Here's Brent's account of what happened on that day.

I remember it being early Super Bowl Sunday and I'm falling in and out of sleep as I realize we have many preparations yet to do for the Super Bowl party we are about to host. We are relatively new to our church, but have been made to feel welcome by our Sunday School class and feel compelled to host a party to get to know fellow members on a more personal level.

As I drifted off to sleep again I saw Katie clearly in a white dress which appeared to be a wedding dress. She told me to have her husband Eric meet with and speak to my neighbor Frank. Frank's wife Jane was in the final stages of brain cancer and my wife Mary cared for her often. Mary is a nurse and has a heart of gold. Frank, like me, is a pilot for Delta and had to travel and could not always be by Jane's side.

I made a general invitation to our Sunday School class of about 20. I didn't get the sense that Eric was a big football fan and I know he had a lot going on. I was genuinely surprised when he came to the party, and knew God made that happen. Knowing God was behind this vision and Eric's attendance at our party, I pulled him aside and told him of my vision of Katie. I described her appearance and that he needed to speak with Frank per Katie's direction.

Eric shared other folks' visions which jibed with my vision. I remember others being pulled into the conversation and while the Saints-Colts game was close many folks didn't care as they were drawn into our conversation. The TV was turned off. People were on the edges of their seats listening to every word Eric was saying about dreams others had had about Katie.

I feel 100% now as I did then that God was behind my Katie experience. I've felt the Holy Spirit's presence in many things in my life but nothing like this vision and the words Katie spoke to me. I never really met Katie as when we moved into town she was consumed by cancer.

*Brent*

## Eric's Observation

I had not really planned on going to Brent's Super Bowl party. Frankly, I am not a big sports fan and I really just wanted to lay low and not be around so many people. I had had people surrounding me for months and was still quite drained by it all. But I began thinking that it might be good for the kids and me just to get out of the house for a while and enjoy ourselves. I figured, free food and a chance to focus on something else like football would be a good way to take our minds off death and cancer.

What seems striking from Brent's dream encounter is this:

Again, the outfit of the resurrected children or bride of Christ is a long white dress, like a wedding dress he described.

What you don't hear in Brent's short description of the encounter is just how stunning it was for me. By this time you might think I was getting used to this sort of accounts, but honestly I wasn't. In fact, I was almost hoping NOT to talk about all this stuff and just veg out to watch some football.

Yet, a moment after I rang his doorbell and we were ushered inside, Brent and his wife Mary approached me with somewhat serious faces and escorted me to the side away from the other guests to have a few words with me.

Mind you, I had never met these people before and had never been in their neighborhood, much less over to their house. Brent began talking first and said he had had a dream with Katie in it. I listened attentively as he said, "First, she just appeared and said to me. 'It's me, Katie. Can you tell Eric that Heaven is wonderful?'"

That stopped me in my tracks. It was almost the identical words Amanda had said when she had her encounter. She was told by Katie that Heaven was wonderful. This is a simple eye-witness account in itself. What was more unique was this time, the person who had the dream was given a message addressed specifically to me. It is interesting that I have never had a dream where Katie appeared directly to me, but that God choose to speak to me through another person.

As Brent kept talking, my attention was wandering as I tried to picture and soak in what I had just been told. It was like a postcard from Heaven. A very short message like, the place is great – wish you were here. See you later.

I had to ask Brent to repeat it all again, and I asked him to describe for me what she looked like. As Brent said, she looked wonderful, like a bride. And then Brent mentioned something about talking to a neighbor. That part seemed foggy to me at the time. I didn't know these folks, let alone any neighbor of theirs. I really didn't see the significance of the neighbor or what that had to do with me.

But then Brent's wife Mary jumped into the conversation. She confirmed that Brent had had this dream and had talked about it the moment they got out of bed. Then she started telling me about the neighbor. I didn't catch the name, but apparently there was a neighbor who had some sort of brain cancer that had effectively left her speechless and paralyzed on one side of her body. Mary started telling me a bit more about the lady and their family and about her husband who was struggling to care for her, but her words were all a blur to me.

I was probably still focusing on the postcard greeting I had just received. The only detail I remembered that night was that this woman who was afflicted with cancer was very angry. So angry that she would hold her breath to let others know how upset she was. I remember thinking what a striking difference this was to my wife who had had little pain, little anger and was frankly pretty calm and spiritual and serene throughout her entire journey.

But the key takeaway to note is this:

God goes after His sheep. Like a good shepherd and He specifically used these circumstances to communicate to me to reach out and comfort others. God is a God of abundant grace and mercy and you will read later how all this played out.

Brent and his wife were surprised when I asked them if they had heard of the other dreams and when they said no, I told all that I was able to share with them that evening. Brent left most of the guests and gathered a small group in his upper living room and turned off the game to hear all these amazing dreams and visions that I have just revealed to you – and he is a huge football fan. Anyhow, it was a powerful time of sharing – so much for vegging out and talking about football. The Lord was on the move again.

When Brent told me about his dream he had that same morning, I knew I was meant to be there.

In the case of all of these collective dream and vision experiences, this was like God leaving a massive clue trail complete with eyewitnesses, video tape clips, photographs, and footprints on earth.

# Chapter Four: God's Trail Of Clues

I call them Hallmarks of God. He showered me with them, especially during my dream, and afterward.

For example, God is loving and is a generous giver. When He acts or blesses He may often do so abundantly or go a bit overboard – as with a lavish gift. Like providing six witnesses when two or three might have been enough.

In the case of all of these collective dream and vision experiences, this was like God leaving a massive clue trail complete with eye witnesses, video tape clips, photographs, and footprints on the earth.

Scripture says reliable testimony is established by two or three witnesses – in this case He doubled those numbers.

This lavish gift of witnesses had extra special meaning to me because of the range of people involved.

Even though Katie and I were highly connected to our church and community with many layers of friends all around us, God chose to reveal these things to people outside of that group. These were not close friends. They were friends and acquaintances of others. We only knew Amanda's family, who attended our church.

The Merritts had joined our Sunday School class near the end of Katie's hospice stay when we were unable to attend our class.

## Other gifts

A major gift from God as a result of my dream was the gift of faith. My perception of an absentee God who made the clock, set it in motion and left it to run by itself, (that is described in the Introduction) was shattered.

I was forced to confront the idea that dreams and visions can and do indeed happen.

I learned expanded meaning of the phrase, God never gives us more than we can handle. More correctly, God never gives us more than we can handle with Him by our side.

He does give us more than we can handle alone, on our own, under our own power.

In fact, that is exactly what He does do. He sends just enough affliction that pushes us beyond what we can handle without Him, so we will turn to Him in our hour of need.

## Angels in Katie's hospice room

Sometimes God orchestrates reminders of His amazing grace long after the fact. A case in point was the revelation by Chaplain Jim Weathers seven years and three months after Katie's passing on to Heaven.

It happened during a spring 2017 Friday morning Log House meeting. When I mentioned to Jim that I was writing a book about all that had happened surrounding Katie's passing, Jim told us that he had talked with Katie about the angels in her hospice room. Remember, Jim played a vital role in our lives and in this story. He was a close friend of mine and paid many visits to us and to Katie, especially once she entered the hospice. Also, it was Jim, if you recall, who knew Janeen Jamison and had asked her to pray for us – leading to Janeen being given her dream/vision experience.

In Jim's words, here's his recollection of that discussion with Katie in hospice:

As Katie neared the day of her departure she began to experience fulfillment of 2 Corinthians 4:16-18 –

[16] Therefore we do not lose heart. Though outwardly we are wasting away, yet inwardly we are being renewed day by day. [17] For our light and momentary troubles are achieving for us an eternal glory that far outweighs them all. [18] So we fix our eyes not on what is seen, but on what is unseen, since what is seen is temporary, but what is unseen is eternal.

The day before her passing as we (Jim and his wife Mary Ann) visited Katie at Southwest Christian Hospice, Katie's expression was very excited as she began to look from one side of the room to the other, visually following movement and expressing great delight. I asked, "Are you seeing something special?"

She responded, "Yes!"

I asked, "Are you seeing angels?"

She replied again with wide-eyed expression, "Yes!"

I asked her to look behind me and tell me if there were two angels standing right behind me. She looked up over my head and said, "Yes!"

I have known that two angels have accompanied me on many ministry occasions and continually are present to minister to me as an heir of salvation. As it says in the first chapter of Hebrews –

[14] Are not all angels ministering spirits sent to serve those who will inherit salvation?

Katie's favorite verse of comfort was Psalm 46:10a, "Be still and know that I am God ...."

Every time I visited with Katie she would have me sing the little chorus:

Be still and know that I am God
Be still and know that I am God
Be still and know that I am God.

She was very comforted by His presence and the visitations which she received in seeing eternal things. Katie knew that she was not going to die, but would depart from the body that had been diminished by disease and would put on another body, one not made with hands, eternal in the heavens. (2 Corinthians 5:1, 2, 8) and she would forever be present with the Lord.

[9] And He said to me, "My grace is sufficient for you, for My strength is made perfect in weakness." Therefore most gladly I will rather boast in my infirmities, that the power of Christ may rest upon me.

# Chapter Five: My Grace Is Sufficient

Katie was well into the physical struggles of the cancer reoccurrence when I had my Road to Damascus dream experience.

Saul, in his experience on the road to Damascus, went from a chief persecutor of Christians to becoming the Apostle Paul, the ultimate defender and proclaimer in faith in the Lord Jesus Christ.

My dream – to me – was my Road to Damascus encounter. It turned my life upside down, and in its wake left me with what the Bible calls *the peace that passeth understanding.*

One of the major results of my dream was being inspired to adopt the phrase or idea that "My grace is sufficient" as my daily theme to live by.

I did not deal with – as Paul did – numerous beatings, ship-wrecks, and imprisonments. Nor have the thorn in the flesh that pained Paul so much that he asked the Lord three times to remove the pain. In the New Testament Paul called that thorn in the flesh a messenger of Satan, whose purpose was to torment Paul, to keep Paul humble, so he would not get puffed up. Most humans directly commissioned by Jesus could very easily let things go to their head, and become haughty.

God, as He had done with Job, allowed Satan to torment Paul for God's own good purpose.

Here is what Paul said about the thorn in the flesh in 2 Corinthians 12:7-10 –

[7] ... Therefore, in order to keep me from becoming conceited, I was given a thorn in my flesh, a messenger of Satan, to torment me. [8] Three times I pleaded with the Lord to take it away from me. [9] But he said to me, "My grace is sufficient for you, for my power is made perfect in weakness." Therefore I will boast all the more gladly about my weaknesses, so that Christ's power may rest on me. [10] That is why, for Christ's sake, I delight in weaknesses, in insults, in hardships, in persecutions, in difficulties. For when I am weak, then I am strong.

My pain involved the anguish because of Katie's cancer, and wanting, praying, hoping the Lord would choose to physically heal

Katie. At the same time Katie and I jointly also prayed that God's will be done.

I believe God chose to give Katie perfect healing by taking her Into God's Country. And doing so in a way that will impact many lives. This is my ultimate reason for writing this book.

Meanwhile, I am constantly reminded:

My grace is sufficient.

Also, my prayer life has grown and changed over the years and through this experience. Many of John Eldredge's books talk about how to pray more effectively and what it is like when God speaks and how He answers prayers.

What I have discovered is that God often answers prayers differently and better than I could have imagined myself. Another thing I have adopted and discovered is that I no longer ask for nearly as many specific things or blessings. Instead, I just raise up my topics of concern, whatever it is that I feel I am in need of help with or any prayer requests of others and I simply present them to God. I no longer go on to suggest an answer or how I might want this to work out. I just present them to God and back off.

I do listen to see if I hear or sense anything immediately. Often I don't hear or receive any word either way, but on many occasions I have heard a simple response. I don't know if I am hearing an audible voice in my ears or just being made to know this simple answer.

What I get back is simply this:

My grace is sufficient. I hear it over and over. Like a comforting reminder from a loving father. I have fully engrained it and know it intuitively.

What usually happens is that over time, I observe the situation, what I prayed about and you know what ... God usually seems to have orchestrated a wonderful answer to my prayers. And it is always better than anything I could have come up with myself.

There is a powerful passage from Philippians 4: 6-7 that I have hung in my bedroom to look at and be reminded of every day:

$^6$ Do not be anxious about anything, but in every situation, by prayer and petition, with thanksgiving, present your requests to God. $^7$ And the peace of God, which transcends all understanding, will guard your hearts and your minds in Christ Jesus.

You know what?

It's true and it works. I am a planner and can get anxious about a lot of things. As an engineer, I prefer to have things well designed and planned out. I am not all that comfortable with the wait-and-see approach. But God has taught me a few things about how He works and how I can indeed trust Him in all things, including the more trivial things as well as the most significant and emotionally stressful things – like cancer.

My advice is to just ask the Lord and leave it at that. Present your petitions and be thankful.

In essence, when I hear God reply, "My grace is sufficient," He is reassuring me of His promise and delivering to me that peace I need to move forward in faith, trusting that our heavenly Father has it all in His hands.

This helps me deal with everything from demands at work, at home and even the stresses that arise simply by living in this stressful and fallen world, and from hearing all the news of the day across the globe. From terrorism to traffic making me late to a meeting – God has it and His grace will be sufficient. No need to panic or speed.

There is usually a sense of closure to my prayers – especially the very important ones of the heart – that happens after I have prayed, and waited and observed that God has answered them in some way.

I enjoy praying to God, to just acknowledge and thank Him for the answered prayer. I never want to take God for granted or fail to acknowledge Him for His graciousness and favor. I know I have probably failed to thank Him many times for blessings I received, simply because of my own ignorance about how many times and ways He blesses me. But when I do pray and thank Him, even that becomes a powerful point of blessing for me.

It often happens like this:

When I reflect back and pray upon giving thanks for the ways God answers prayers, I marvel about how wonderfully He has shown up and answered my prayers. He and I seem to have this little set of questions, almost like a brief dialog between a grateful child and his father. I simply ask two questions:

First, "Lord, you are able to do these things?" To which He replies, "Yes, I can." This always reassures me of God's power and skill. He is ABLE to do all things.

Second, I ask perhaps the more important question. "Yes, Lord, but you are willing to do these things ... for me?" And without hesitation, He replies, "Yes, I am." This always melts my heart and causes a lump of gratitude and emotion to swell up in my throat. This gives me a second reassurance, not just of God's capability to do all things, but His willingness to do them for me. He is WILLING to give these good gifts to His children

These are humbling things, because often I feel so truly unworthy to receive such blessings. Who am I that the Lord of the universe should pay such attention to me? And yet He does.

This makes my love for the Lord well up inside. It feels like that passage where Jesus says He can give us water that will well up inside us and overflow. That is how this kind of prayer of thanksgiving feels. You should develop this habit – for it is eternally gratifying – for both you and the Lord. I am certain the Lord loves a cheerful giver and a thankful receiver. It is a joy to acknowledge and give thanks for what God has done for us in our lives.

As we tried to fight the tendency to imagine the worst case scenario – that this could be very serious, even fatal – we noticed that suddenly our world looked very different. We no longer worried about the same things. We had new and much bigger issues that took center stage.

# Chapter Six: Twilight Time

Our story really began when things started to change and the first cracks of a new reality began to appear. That happened four years before my dream.

When it comes to cancer, you are able to look back and remember precisely when your story took its first turn down a new and dark path. It is when you first hear the word *cancer*; first feel something unusual, or are told, "Hmmm – that looks suspicious; we had better check that out."

I remember how it felt when our story began – like we were walking through a haze, gingerly stepping in unfamiliar territory. The low-lying mist surrounding us obscured all sorts of potentially dangerous obstacles. The first time we even heard the C word, it did not fully register. Our minds could not even grasp the magnitude of all that it could or would mean to us. Just thinking about it made our heads spin, like being awoken abruptly from sleep. The best way I can think to describe it is that it felt like waking up in the middle of twilight – or perhaps even in the old TV show *The Twilight Zone*.

The twilight period is still the best way I know to describe how those early days felt. Twilight is that strange portion of the day where it is not quite light out, but it is not dark either. This *in-between* period is a strange and disorienting time of day when you are not sure whether you are asleep or awake; whether the things you see are real or a figment of your imagination. You may wonder if something is lurking in the darkness or is it just your eyes and imagination playing tricks on you. It is a time to move cautiously and look carefully around at the strange shadows created during twilight.

Another reason I call this the twilight period in our story is that it felt like things could go either way – they could get brighter or darker.

Actual twilight occurs two times a day – at sunrise and again at sunset.

Experiencing twilight can be very beautiful and peaceful. I love to watch the sky turn colors and fade to black, especially if I can watch the sunset over a lake or the ocean. Morning twilight can also be wonderful, watching the sky slowly brighten and the world take shape and come to life as the first direct rays of sun stream across the sky.

At other times, twilight can feel like a dangerous and confusing period.

Commuting early in the morning – especially in a strange place – can be tricky. Navigation becomes difficult with the sunrise. The sky begins to brighten, but the light and shadows can play tricks on your eyes, making it difficult to see important obstacles or other dangers. Turning away from the shadows into the sun can cause you to be blinded as you try to make out the pathway ahead.

Driving in the evening is also more dangerous as the sun goes down, leaving shadows that can absorb bits of light in ways that can confuse a driver.

I learned more about the dangers of twilight during my training in the U.S. Army. Officers taught us that the most difficult – yet most important – time to be alert and to watch out for an attack from the enemy is during twilight.

Opponents attack during twilight due to the vulnerability brought to those in danger. It is also when defending soldiers are apt to be the most tired and at their weakest. The element of surprise from the attacker is intensified if you are disoriented due to the trickery of the light.

I remember participating in a field training exercise where we were paired up with another soldier who became our foxhole buddy.

As a buddy team, it meant that anytime our platoon stopped advancing, the two of us would work together to prepare a fighting position. If this occurred at night, our buddy team would build a more elaborate and deep foxhole in which to hide and rest.

We spent the entire night digging and improving our foxhole fighting position. One of us would dig while the other kept watch for enemy movement. By the time dawn approached, we had been up most of the night, and we had managed to create a fairly deep and well-concealed foxhole.

In the wee hours of the morning, we finished our digging and had hunkered down. Then we attempted to alternate getting some rest and keeping watch. As the dawn approached, the sky turned an eerie color and the forest took on a daunting hue. Shadows reached out in every direction, and it was difficult to make out anything in the dim light.

As we were about to learn, twilight was the most dangerous time of the day. My buddy and I were very tired and worn out. Between the sleep deprivation and the shifting shadows, our eyes were playing tricks on us. We struggled to tell whether we were seeing or hearing enemy movement in the bushes around us, or whether it was just our imagination.

A staccato of shots pierced the silence. Our entire fighting position was quickly overrun by teams of attacking soldiers who had sprung up from startlingly close positions right in front of us. We had no clue that the enemy had indeed been sneaking up on us and lurking so close.

I was glad this was only an exercise using blank ammunition and not an actual enemy with real bullets. Had the situation been real, we would have died quickly. It gave me new awareness and respect for the dangers of the twilight period.

Those are very different views of twilight. One is a very positive view, complete with images of lounge chairs near the ocean, while the other is a very negative view, filled with images of disorientation and battle.

Those were the contrasting outlooks we contemplated as we awaited news about the cancer. We hoped for relief and serenity, yet we feared hardship and suffering. What we felt must be similar to the feelings of a prize fighter as he receives a hard blow to the head. The impact of the blow sends the boxer reeling in pain as he sees stars before his eyes and his world is spinning out of control. As he recoils, he begins to frantically reach out and grab onto something to regain balance and composure.

Can you relate to my word picture?

Have you ever faced adversity, or even the threat of adversity, such as a cancer *false alarm*, or a dreaded call from the police that there has been an accident?

As we tried to fight the tendency to imagine the worst case scenario – that this could be very serious, even fatal – we noticed that suddenly our world looked very different. We no longer worried about the same things. We had new and much bigger issues that took center stage.

The *familiar* seemed foreign to us.

Our surroundings looked dangerous and eerie. It felt like someone had jolted us awake in the middle of a twilight as we attempted to determine which twilight we were experiencing.

Was this the morning twilight where our world was about to get brighter, less scary, and more uplifting?

Or was it the evening twilight where our world was about to get darker, more shadowy, and less secure?

For us, twilight first began quietly one evening when my wife said she felt something odd, a small lump the size of a marble in her breast. No warning – just a small irregularity, nothing major or painful, that she happened to discover while laying down to sleep one night. That was the start. It had crept in like a thief in the night.

After a day or two of confirming that something felt unusual, the process started as we began checking with the doctor, seeing a specialist, getting a mammogram, discussing the results, having a biopsy, and getting second opinions.

Already it was beginning to feel like a scary roller-coaster ride, one we soon hoped would come to a stop so we could get off, never to ride again.

Throughout the twilight time, we felt like we were stuck in an agonizing fog of confusion and distress, not knowing whether to start worrying about cancer, or to remain calm, hoping it was a false alarm. The uncertainty of the twilight period finally ended on that fateful day when we heard the results of the biopsy: cancer.

Our world was shaken, ambushed by a six-letter word.

I imagine this terrible twilight period is similar to what it must feel like if you are waiting in a hospital after a loved one has been in a serious accident. You eagerly await good news while fearing it might be bad news.

For us, this period was a very difficult and revealing time. All the while, our feelings ran the full gamut of emotions as we tried to hold it all inside, trying not to panic but also trying not to be in denial about what was happening. We wanted to share our burden and concern with others, but we also did not want to alarm them. We felt as though we rode a teeter-totter up and down, from panic to controlled calm. We wanted to be strong in our faith, and yet we wanted to scream and run away in fear.

Another aspect of our journey was our role as parents. Our two children were in first and third grades. The last thing we wanted to do was try to explain the risks and potential outcomes of a dreaded disease like cancer to our children.

Our parenting instinct was to keep this news under wraps. It felt like a time to be tough, to keep our emotions under control and out of sight, because we did not want to unnecessarily scare the children, and we did not want to camp out there emotionally ourselves.

It was an agonizing time when we simultaneously wanted to shut down and do nothing, yet at the same time, we also wanted things to speed up and move quickly through the testing process. To cope, we found ourselves trying to focus on anything else we could, trying to busy our minds and our lives to avoid thinking about the worst.

I was startled, because that was precisely the same thought I had, and I would have said it in exactly the same words. We did not know what to expect, but we had a palpable sense that God was doing something in us, to us, or through us.

# Chapter Seven: Adjusting the Compass

In the early stages of twilight, God had also crept in on a whisper.

By that I mean, the first time we sensed God at work through this experience was so subtle, we barely recognized it. It happened at some point in the middle of our twilight period, between initial observation and the final diagnosis of breast cancer.

I was actually very pleased that during this intense period of six or seven days, we both were eager and able to pray to the Lord separately and together about the situation.

One day when Katie and I were praying together, a most unusual thing happened. We were asking the Lord for the most obvious request: to spare us from cancer – to remove, to cleanse, to heal any abnormality and allow us to avoid this cancer scare altogether. I remember using some of the same words Christ used when He prayed in the Garden of Gethsemane shortly before His arrest and crucifixion. I echoed Christ's words and asked God if this bitter cup of cancer could pass from our lips.

Like Christ, we had the sense to qualify the prayer with our deepest desire when we stated, "Thy will be done."

We were also hoping and asking that His will would be in agreement with our desire to avoid the cancer. We paused, waited and listened. I was not prepared for, nor had I ever experienced, what happened next.

I cannot say that I heard something, but what I sensed is hard to describe. Immediately, Katie and I exchanged glances with a peculiar look in our eyes. Without even articulating the thought in my head before speaking, I asked her, "Do you feel something?"

"Yes," she answered.

"So do I," I said.

After a pause, I asked her, "What do you feel?"

I was frankly a bit unsure and hesitant to share, so I chickened out by asking her to share her thoughts first – I just wasn't quite ready to go out on a limb and say what I felt in case it was different from what she felt.

She said, "I feel that God is IN this."

I was startled, because that was precisely the same thought I had, and I would have said it in exactly the same words. We did not know what to expect, but we had a palpable sense that God was doing something in us, to us, or through us.

The silence was broken with a second prayer we both prayed that was meant to supersede the first.

"Lord, we know that you are doing something in us or through us, and whatever it is, we ask that you not take IT away."

We meant what we were saying in that second prayer – that even if God healed Katie as we initially asked and we would not have to go through the cancer experience, we did not want God to take away whatever good He was doing in us. In fact, we even believed this second prayer was necessary especially if the first prayer to remove the cancer were to be answered, because we had this sense that if the cancer news was a false alarm, there was a very good chance that we would just revert back to who we were prior to feeling a lump. We felt that we were more likely to miss out on what God was doing if we were healed, than if we were not immediately healed. In any case, we knew that whatever IT was that God was doing was going to fulfill His purpose in our lives and yield a huge blessing to each of us – a blessing that neither of us wanted to miss out on.

This shared sense or prompting to pray the second prayer was what was really odd. I am not sure if I had ever felt compelled or prayed that kind of prayer before, ever. I suppose it was a prayer of surrender based on some unseen sense of assurance – like God had already told us to be still and not worry, because He was in this. One of Katie's favorite and simple passages from scripture are the words "Be still and know that I am God."

It also felt like it was a very small, still kind of prompting or hearing from God – like what is described in 1 Kings when the Lord spoke, not in the wind, or an earthquake, or the fire, but in a *gentle whisper* that assured us that He was in this and we could ask Him to continue the good work that He had started.

That was the start of everything that was to follow. We did have to drink the bitter cup of cancer, yet He did honor and answer our second, but deeper prayer. He showed us what IT was and brought to pretty full completion the work He intended to do with IT.

I believe God honored that prayer by all that He brought us to and through and continues to honor it to this day in the writing of this book. This is not a book that I could have written on my own. I am merely recounting all that God took me through.

He is still fulfilling and honoring that prayer: that the good work that He intended is still playing out, affecting the lives of others, drawing them to Him, revealing God's glory and goodness.

It is an honor and a privilege that is hard to put words to. I just am humbled to be a part of IT.

We could not have articulated it then, but looking back on it several years later, it was as if each of our hearts had a compass attached to it, like the deck of a sailing ship may have a compass mounted on it. The captain navigates the ship by setting the dials of the compass to establish the direction and path of the ship. We sensed God reaching inside our hearts and making a few adjustments to our compasses. He was not making massive changes – we were pretty *good* Christians already. We were quite active in our church and had been for many years. We were sincere in our practice of the faith and genuinely wanted to follow the Lord. However, I do think there was still a *shallowness* to our faith. I doubt if we were really whole-hearted in the pursuit of our faith. We were sometimes hot, sometimes cold, but basically lukewarm much of the time. We were using our heads but not engaging with the Lord at the deepest heart level.

Yes, God was making fine adjustments to the settings on the compasses of our hearts. If you know much about compasses on ships or planes, you understand that even minor changes to a setting can have a major impact on the trajectory and the ultimate destination of the ship or plane.

These adjustments were meant to change the path and final destination of our hearts and lives. And that is exactly what happened. The course of our next five years – and I also believe the course of our lives in eternity – was significantly changed and impacted by those heart adjustments.

Everything that God took us through in the next five years deepened and broadened our faith in ways that could not have happened otherwise.

The result of increased dependence on God is something that I eventually came to call *The Luxury of Cancer*.

I know that phrase sounds like a contradiction in terms. How can anything about cancer be considered a luxury?

# Chapter Eight: The Luxury of Cancer

As our life filled with doctor's appointments, and our network of friends began to gather around us, I noticed something about myself and others in this new and radically different world of affliction. We were unusually calm with our focus first and foremost on one thing:

Our relationship and dependence on God. This is not something everyone experiences or turns to. You see all sorts of reactions from people when adversity strikes and it is often in such situations that people can see or reveal to themselves and others just what they put their trust in and where they stand in their faith journey.

The result of increased dependence on God is something that I eventually came to call *The Luxury of Cancer*.

I know that phrase sounds like a contradiction in terms. How can anything about cancer be considered a luxury? Believe me it was no picnic – it was really hard. But, from another prospective it was a luxury. Let me explain.

This period made us consider many things – especially where, or from whom, we would find help. I realized that, throughout our lives, we all end up facing an array of different challenges and adversities. When a crisis happens, the first thing we typically do is consider the options of how we will respond to the situation.

Take, for example, the difficulty of job loss. If we have been blessed with savings, we may be able to turn to our bank account and live off that money for a while. This gives us a feeling of being able to handle the situation on our own without need of others or God.

However, the longer we go without work, we start realizing we may need help from others. We may first turn to a headhunter or employment agency to help us find another job. If none comes along quickly, we may turn to the government to apply for unemployment in order to keep money coming while continuing our search for another job.

We may turn to our investment manager and cash in stocks to keep food on the table. We might be able to turn to our family for relief while we go through this rough patch in our career. Eventually, we might have to move in with friends or relatives to get by. So, depending on our circumstances and resources, we may have a wide range of options to turn to in our hour of need to rescue us from whatever challenge comes our way.

The same is also true for other kinds of adversity or challenges. We may have a range of options at our disposal when we are faced with a major life challenge.

If we have:

    marriage problems, we call a counselor, or a lawyer;
    back problems, we consult a doctor or chiropractor;
    sagging body, we can see a trainer or a plastic surgeon;
    relational issues, we talk with a shrink;
    bad hair, we go to a stylist.

With cancer, things are different. No matter how much money you have or whether you have access to the best doctors in the world, there is no guarantee that they can do you any good. Nothing, including personal resources, experience, family, friends, or professional contracts can cure your cancer and solve your problems. They can help, but there is no delusion of a guarantee that they can find a solution.

Unlike most other forms of adversity, with cancer you are much less tempted to trust your other sources, and much more likely to turn to God for help.

I call these other sources our *lesser gods*. We may not think of them as gods, but in many ways they can become like modern versions of the carved idols that more primitive societies worship. These are dead gods of wood, rather than a living God of the Spirit. These household idols were believed to be the link to the source of some divine power that could possibly be harnessed to help deal with earthly problems.

I wonder how much *modern man* has made a god out of various secular resources or even our government. Most of us have our carefully constructed safety network of doctors, lawyers, insurance policies, savings, wealth, family, friends, even our fellow church members that we plan to turn to when the chips are down. Others work to create a national government that is able to serve as our safety network – Medicare, Social Security, unemployment, FEMA – whatever may happen to us, many look to the government for their assistance and salvation.

Though some challenges may indeed be able to be met *on our own* through these resources, when that happens our self-reliance seems to be strengthened. If we are not careful, we will put our faith in these *lesser gods* to be our saviors instead of turning to Almighty God, the Highest Authority, for our strength and help.

So, for these reasons, cancer was a kind of luxury because it helped us skip past all of that. You don't give your money or your lawyer a try – cancer brings you straight to God. The right path is suddenly very clear. And often, not in a moment too soon, because cancer can move quickly, you will need all the insight, guidance, and strength that only God can put into your heart to get you through what is to come. As I write this, Houston has just experienced what was described as the most costly natural disaster in American history and the state of Florida was undergoing hurricane Irma, the most powerful storm in the Atlantic ever. Lots of people are about to go through hardship and it will be revealing who they turn to and whom they trust during this season of trouble. Scripture says, in this world you will have trouble, but take heart for I have overcome the world. I pray people come to discover and truly grasp this truth.

So, with cancer – and hopefully with other similar dangerous and disastrous times – in your life, perhaps for the first time, you are finally up against something that no one on earth is guaranteed to fix. You realize that only God has the power to take on a menace as pernicious as cancer. This may be the first time in the lives of many where we finally choose to turn to God with our whole heart. This is true in all circumstances. However, with cancer it happens a whole lot faster. In an odd way, this is a luxury.

How many of us really turn to God first?

In fact, don't most of us think of turning to God as the last resort, rather than the first and best option?

I mean, really, isn't this how we live most of the time? We have this unspoken policy with God that says, "OK, God, I will handle most of what comes my way, and You take care of things up there. I will consult with You only when I have to."

It is only when the do-it-yourself approach fails that we finally turn to God, and He can begin to do business with us. He can finally begin to *speak* to us, teach us, help us, and heal us. The Bible says in various places in Matthew, John and the book of Acts that when we finally turn to God, He will truly heal us. In Matthew 13:14-16 Jesus talked about the people to whom He spoke parables, saying, [14] In them is fulfilled the prophecy of Isaiah:

"'You will be ever hearing but never understanding;
   you will be ever seeing but never perceiving.
[15] For this people's heart has become calloused;
   they hardly hear with their ears,
   and they have closed their eyes.
Otherwise they might see with their eyes,
   hear with their ears,
   understand with their hearts
and turn, and I would heal them.'

[16] But blessed are your eyes because they see, and your ears because they hear."

Healing comes – though maybe not in the way we think it should happen – when we seek God with our whole hearts. God said in Jeremiah 29:13 (NKJV), "And you will seek Me and find Me, when you search for Me with all your heart."

Can we see this struggle in ourselves and in our approach to life? When we handle life on our own we apparently walk around most of the time with our eyes blinded, our ears stopped up, and our hearts deadened; we cannot see, hear, or understand. Perhaps that is why life can seem so confusing and God can seem to be so distant. It is not God who departed or got further away; it is us walking around with our eyes blinded, ears closed, and hearts deadened.

I love the verse in 2 Corinthians 3:16 (NKJV) that says, "Nevertheless when one turns to the Lord, the veil is taken away."

It is only when we TURN to Him, that He can begin to show us, tell us, and open our hearts to be truly healed. Healing and restoration – that is what it is all about.

I tell people at the end of the journey, that the man I was five years prior, before we began our cancer journey, is not the same man I am today. That man could never have gotten through what I just went through. God had taught me so much and trained me up in preparation for what He knew would come.

# Chapter Nine: Roots and Branches

The coming months and years were amazingly hard and amazingly good. The first sentence in the literary classic, *A Tale of Two Cities* by Charles Dickens comes to mind:
It was the best of times, it was the worst of times.

For us, it was both.

The difficult journey that caused us to be *frequent flyers* in all sorts of medical offices included a double mastectomy, reconstruction surgery, chemotherapy, follow-up treatments, side effects, and lifestyle change. It was a very unwelcome and difficult year – you could call it hell. There were, however, amazing periods of growth as well. In fact, during the difficult first year in the battle with cancer, we had incredible blessings and opportunities to learn more about God and grow in His likeness and stature.
What did the growth and blessing look like?
I like to use the analogy of a tree. Katie was like a tree planted near a stream as it is described in Jeremiah 17:7-8:

"But blessed is the man who trusts in the LORD, whose confidence is in Him. He will be like a tree planted by the water that sends out its roots by the stream. It does not fear when heat comes; its leaves are always green. It has no worries in a year of drought and never fails to bear fruit."

Katie's roots got very deep. She seemed to dig in spiritually and tap deep into the source of strength and encouragement that was inexhaustible. Almost by instinct, I saw her get more involved in Bible study, and it was a joy to see her relationships with other women, spiritual sisters of the faith, grow and deepen.
For me, I suppose I also was like a tree planted by a river. Only what would have been more observable about my changes was that it was more like my branches grew larger and broadened

out. A tree cannot support larger branches unless the roots beneath the soil are also growing and up to the task.

I branched out deeper and wider – reading, taking and teaching classes, leading men's groups and Bible studies. The biggest source of development and outlet for that growth was, by far, my exposure and immersion into the works of author John Eldredge. His works, more than any other source, were the means that God reached me, taught my soul, and prepared my spirit for what was to come ahead.

I tell people at the end of the journey, that the man I was five years prior, before we began our cancer journey, is not the same man I am today. That man could never have gotten through what I just went through. God had taught me so much and trained me up in preparation for what He knew would come.

## A small prompting

The story of how God protected me and prepared me for what was to come started with a whisper from a still small voice inside. Isn't it true that, when we look back on the start of what turned out to be a major turning point in our lives, that it often turned on what felt like a tiny trifle – a small, seemingly insignificant decision that turned out to be the turning point that led to all that would follow?

This whisper also came unexpectedly, out of left field, in the form of a prompting to pull together a group of guys and form a men's group for someone else. This ended up being one of the ways God first began to act upon our twilight prayer when we requested of God not to take away the good work in our hearts that He had already begun.

Mind you, I had never led a men's group and frankly never had the urge to lead one. We had been in couples groups that were mostly social gatherings among church friends where we did some light church-based study. Leading or hosting, on the other hand, was not something I had much interest, skill, or experience with. Still, I felt this strange prompting to do this for a friend. He was our family physician and neighbor. During a recent driveway conversation, he seemed really rundown and burdened by the stress of life and his job. Somehow, I felt I was *supposed* to get some men together to give him a space to talk about his concerns, vent about issues, and just hang out with some guys.

I don't know if you have noticed this, but it is not that common for men to join groups or hang out to simply talk and support each other. Some guys play sports together, but it is fairly common for men to not have many close friends or at least to not have a group of guys to go to with life's challenges. We are often like lone rangers; we don't like to ask for directions, and we don't want to sit around and share our feelings. We prefer to be *tough* and figure life out on our own.

As such, it felt quite odd for me to even think of such an idea. Yet, for some reason, I sensed it was from God; this was long before I acknowledged that sensing things from God was possible. Remember, I always took God for that genius clockmaker who set the world in motion and was off on vacation, letting everything happen on auto-pilot. The idea of hearing or sensing anything from God, especially any kind of prompting or instructions, was simply not a category I thought about.

Yet, there it was – a small, simple request from God to step out and start a group. I half-heartedly called a few of my friends and asked if they would be at all interested in getting together one morning a week. When they responded that they were interested, I was so surprised that I thought, "Really? Why?" I did not say that out loud or to them, but it is what I was thinking. I really thought the guys would not be interested or not want to bother to get up early one morning a week, and then I could drop the idea of a men's group and put the matter to rest.

However, when seven or eight guys said yes, I had a dilemma on my hands. I realized that since I was the one that pulled them together, I was going to have to be the one to lead this thing. To make matters worse, I needed to have a plan, a program, or something. I mean, what would we possibly talk about? Men do not usually just sit around and talk like the ladies often can.

As I stressed about what to do, I thought of all the religious books and speakers I had read or heard in the past. Working for a

company like Chick-fil-A that was founded on Christian principles, I was surrounded by plenty of committed Christians and
exposed to lots of good books by Christian authors.

I had a stack of books on my nightstand table in my *to-read*
pile. I was into a number of good contemporary authors, such as
Bill Hybles, John Ortberg, and Bruce Wilkinson. But, as I thought
about which one to use for starting a men's group, suddenly I
remembered one book in particular: *Wild at Heart* by a relatively
unknown author at the time, John Eldredge.

Interestingly, I had been given the book by a colleague. He
told me that it was a book that lots of guys related to and found
inspiring. However, after skimming the first couple of chapters, I
had set it aside in favor of some deeper works by other more
intellectual writers that appealed more to me. Honestly, my initial
pass through the first couple of chapters left me thinking, "So
what, some rugged outdoorsy guy finds God out in nature – big
deal! That's his story, not mine." (Even though I am an Eagle
Scout and former Army officer.)

I felt the book just did not speak to me, especially compared
with works from the great authors like C.S. Lewis, for example. I
preferred to learn more details about God, not hear about how one
guy discovered God in nature or something like that. But there I
was, faced with the challenge of bringing together a group of guys
for the benefit of one man in the group, and I needed something
that we all might relate to. I was desperate, and *Wild at Heart* was
all that came to mind. Desperate times call for desperate measures,
I thought. Fine, we will study Eldredge's book.

What happened next surprised me more than anyone else.
The group formed, and we began meeting in the local Chick-fil-A
restaurant one morning a week before work. To my surprise, the
guys seemed to be into it. In fact, after about three or four weeks,
so was I. This group came suddenly to life. I had never imagined
it would really stay together, but with each passing week and
chapter, we were all getting more and more into the book, and
enjoying the company of other men on a regular basis.

After about a month came a second surprise. The guy whom I felt led to start the group for in the first place, my friend the physician, told me he was not able to attend any longer. He said he had been struggling to attend in the morning before work because this was an important time for him to research issues for his patients. He expressed thanks and regret, but made it clear that he had to leave the group. I was shocked – the only guy to drop out was the guy for whom the group was created.

Even though praying or talking to God about things was a very odd and new thing for me, I remember asking God out loud, "What's the deal? I thought this was something you asked me to do for him. Why is he leaving?"

I heard nothing in reply, just silence. I began to wonder why I formed the group in the first place. I thought – so much for any kind of *prompting* from above. I figured we would at least finish out the book study and see what happened after that. I assumed the group would soon drift apart.

That's when the really big surprise hit. Within another week or two my wife was diagnosed with breast cancer. Our world was turned upside down, and she and I entered the twilight period that I described earlier.

The group kept meeting and an amazing thing happened. I realized that this group of guys that I had gathered together to be there for someone else, turned out to be a group of friends who were there for me in my hour of need.

In fact, the guys became much tighter. It was as if they circled the wagons and rallied around me. I had never had many close friends before, and now these guys were right there for me, ready to listen, to help out, or just to stand alongside me as my world was spinning into a tailspin. These men became my *band of brothers* – a core group that I could talk with, share with, and even cry with about this terrible development. Like Job who had his close friends, I had close friends to simply be with me, mourn with me, and fight with me.

I did not know what was about to happen next in my life, but God did. He was already at work, reaching out, preparing a way, and providing the grace and the means for us to get through it. This is God's heart and will toward all His children. God started showing me that it was Him who was at work first, He who brought these men around me and He who would be my source of strength and foundation for what lay ahead.

My small act of obedience to help another came back to me tenfold. Had I not listened to that still small voice, I would have lost out on a mountain of blessings. As I would find out, this principle has come true again and again. And the blessing, the rewarding feeling you received from being obedient and responding to God's prompting – well, it is worth its weight in gold. In fact, isn't that perhaps what it means in scripture when God implores us to store up for ourselves treasure in Heaven – where moth and rust does not destroy it?

We are blessed to be a blessing and we receive blessings as we bless others. God's economy works on these simple principles of love and generosity, reaping and sowing. It all works together for good for those who trust in the Lord. Try it yourself, test the Lord on this. I am certain you will not be disappointed.

How strange it would be for someone to say, "Hey, I just had a dream that you are going to die soon; but don't worry, it was a really, really good dream and I feel such a relief, don't you?"

# Chapter Ten: Telling Katie About My Dream

Two weeks after my dream, I told Katie about it. There were reasons for the delay. Right after I received the dream, I was so blown away by the experience and the content, I really first wanted immediate interpretation from close spiritual friends.

The timing of the dream was perfect, as only God can deliver perfect.

First of all, it came on Sept 18 – which is my actual birthday. So, in that sense, it was like a birthday gift to me from the Lord.

Secondly, it was a Friday, which is when I routinely attend my Log House men's group for Bible study. As soon as I got my kids up and ready for school, I went to the Log House where I knew my spiritually-deep friends – I was sure – would help me understand and process this dream.

I was quite certain about the underlying clear message of the dream – that Katie would be leaving (dying) soon and that she would be going to Heaven. But I needed input from someone with more experience in biblical matters than I to help unpack all that I received.

Frankly, I had some obvious concerns about the dream. While it gave me great comfort and peace to receive the message and assurance, it was still bad news – my wife would not be here much longer. I was keenly aware that this would be hard news for lots of people to hear – most especially my wife. I could see the contradictory message of the dream and could imagine how bizarre my words might sound to anyone else.

How strange it would be for someone to say, "Hey, I just had a dream that you are going to die soon; but don't worry, it was a really, really good dream and I feel such a relief, don't you?"

I mean, I knew what I had experienced and I felt the instant relief of all sadness – that peace that passes all understanding, and the wiping away of every tear.

But I now felt that relief precisely because I experienced or underwent the encounter. It was literally like going into and recovering from surgery. While a procedure eliminated most of your pain, it is not really possible for anyone else to know that experience for themselves personally like you do. It was very much an individual and personal experience. I had enough sense to realize that this may not sound very happy or hopeful to anyone else, least of whom would be my wife.

So, I paused and prayed about it. I mean, I couldn't NOT tell her, but the question was whether to tell her now or at some time in the future when her passing was more obvious or imminent. I asked the Lord, should I reveal this now, or later? I came to the conclusion that I should hold off until I felt a prompting. It would be odd to keep such a powerful spiritual experience to myself, but I had already had the chance to share and vent the experience with my guys in my band of brothers at the Log House. That could be enough for a while. I figured that timing was important and that the Lord would prompt me when *now* was the right time.

Two weeks after my dream, I sensed the opportunity to share it. Typically on Sunday evenings, after the kids were down to sleep, my wife and I would let our guard down among ourselves and just voice the thoughts of our heart. At these times, there was not a need to be strong at all times or put on a courageous face, we could just be ourselves.

Something she said that evening sounded pretty down and I just wanted to pass along my dream story to give her some sort of a boost. So I simply said I had something of great comfort to share with her, and I told her the experience as it unfolded for me.

She sat and listened patiently and quietly and when I finished, I looked up at her and her immediate reaction was, "Where is the comfort in that?!"

I realized my fear had been correct – that this would not sound comforting to others, especially her. Yet, I had prayed about when to share it, and had prayed that when I did, it would be a source of comfort to her.

Not really knowing what to say or do, I simply repeated the dream. I hoped that perhaps on a second pass, I could somehow get across the peace and comfort it provided me with the hope that it would somehow give her peace as well.

Strangely, I think it did.

After my second telling of the same story, she seemed to quietly accept it. I don't know what God may have done inside her head or her heart to make her accept this abrupt news with such peace and grace, but I think God must have done something in her. I was relieved to have the dream off my chest and that she seemed to accept and perhaps even start to draw some comfort from it.

Another important, and most likely spiritually-prompted conversation between us occurred not long after I shared the dream. It was another Sunday evening and we were lying next to each other in bed talking about things – sometimes trivial things and sometimes heart-wrenching topics like the future for the kids.

We were laying there peacefully when she abruptly said, "You will find someone."

I replied, "What?" – not entirely sure what she meant.

She told me, "After I'm gone, you will find someone to be your wife."

It caught me off guard. Frankly, I had no desire to have this conversation. At this point, her symptoms were starting to worsen, but they had not been radically worse. There was no telling how long she might survive the disease. But I suspected the reality and the trust in the dream I had shared had begun to sink in for her and she was already accepting her own passing as something in the near or foreseeable future.

I tried to change the subject because it felt unnecessary, premature and unpleasant. We did not have to go there. But she seemed insistent and repeated her words – that I would find someone new. So, realizing that I was not going to be able to just change subjects that easily, I said what I assumed would be the most appropriate and reassuring thing that I could in this situation. Knowing how much she loved being a mom and how important the children were to her, I replied, "OK, but I will be sure someone new is good with the kids."

By this time in the disease process, she was somewhat weak and typically spoke softly and slowly, but she responded quite forcefully and energetically. She sat fully up and turned to look directly at me and said, "No, she doesn't have to be good for the kids – she has to be good for YOU!"

I was stunned to hear these words – my wife telling me to find someone new and telling me to put myself ahead of the needs of our kids. Remember they were seven and ten years old.

She continued. "The kids are more than half-way grown – you need someone who will be good for you."

Too stunned to speak, I felt a lump form in my throat and didn't exactly know how to respond. I wanted to protest, to not make this about me, and just say what seemed most appropriate and comforting to her, but I just couldn't seem to find any words to say other than a quiet, "OK."

I am not sure if I had ever felt her love more poignantly than at that moment. Even compared with our wedding day and every day in-between, this felt like a deep love. In effect, she was setting me free – free to move on with my life after she was gone and free to find someone for me. I look back at that moment as a very profound and almost mysteriously holy moment.

In time, and what turned out to be a short time, God did lead me to another woman, Clara, whom I dated for a year and married about a year-and-a-half after Katie's passing. I look back to that conversation as a pivotal moment – a sort of fond letting go that was bitter and sweet at the same time. She gave me permission to find love again and not live in the past, stuck longing for her after she had gone. I am not sure most people have the heart or strength of character to have that conversation.

Four minutes into a rated G movie and I am crying quietly in the darkness of the movie theater, trying not to show my sadness to anyone else, especially my wife and kids, whom we took there to get some relief from heavy subjects like disease and death.

# Chapter Eleven: Up Is Down

Not long after that conversation with Katie, we took the kids out and each was allowed to bring one friend with us to see a movie.

In that season of cancer, even going to the movies was hard. When you go to the movies, often you want to just be entertained and to take a break from the cares and concerns of real life. The desire for a little harmless escape from reality is all the more intense when you are in the middle of a life struggle like final stage cancer. Both the patient and the immediate caregiver long for some kind of break.

But so many movies also have themes that would make them difficult to watch. Any movies with death or cancer touched on a sore spot, and movies that showcased too much of life that you can no longer do or look forward to, can be a downer. This already eliminates a lot of movies. In those days we tried hard to pick the kind of movies that would be upbeat – like a comedy or drama that does not look like it will be a tearjerker that belongs on the Hallmark Channel.

So we went out to see the newest Pixar movie titled simply Up. I figured it should be a safe choice – it was a G-rated movie and was a cartoon. I reasoned this would be a great movie free of emotional landmines and, frankly, a movie we could bring the kids to where I might even nod off and get some sleep in the darkened theater. During these days, I always felt tired, run-down as the primary caregiver. It seemed almost all of our lives revolved around the disease and caring for Katie and the kids.

Little did I know that the opening scene gives the backstory to the main character, who when the movie actually opened, was a grumpy old man who lived alone in his house. The backstory that whizzed by in pictures with a musical soundtrack and narrator told his life story – it showed a young boy who grows and marries his high school sweetheart.

The montage continues showing their dream of traveling the world, but the major events in their life were always eating into the piggy bank where they were trying to save funds so they could go on a fantastic world trip. The scenes of their life advanced, showing the wedding, their careers, the purchase of their first house, the birth of their children, the enlargement of their house, their mutual, shared interests.

Then the slide show reveals a turn of events. The wife is shown getting sick and eventually dying and being buried and the old man being alone and miserable, putting his dreams and the savings bank on the shelf, as he settled into being an unhappy old man – alone in his old house, never having taken the adventure trip that they had dreamed about all those years

I was undone in my seat.

Four minutes into a rated-G movie and I am crying quietly in the darkness of the movie theater, trying not to show my sadness to anyone else, especially my wife and kids, whom we took there to get some relief from heavy subjects like disease and death.

I couldn't believe that this was the story I had stumbled into. Instead of sleeping through the movie, I watched the entire show with great interest, and without spoiling the movie, let's just say the ending was a positive one for the character, but brought around a second round of tears for me. It was bitter sweet. So, again, I had to rely upon my dream and the positive experience it gave me and my trust in the Lord to help get me through the hard things like this.

When I say the dream dealt with most of my anger and hurt, it did not deal with 100%. There were still hard times – like this one that crept up on me in the movie theater when I would least expect it. There were other times like this, but each time I had this well-grounded sense that God was with us and all would be well.

Just as I was ready to leave home, my cell phone rings and it is Jamie Bosworth, a good friend and leader of my men's Log House Bible study. After greeting him, I was shocked to hear him say in the most causal and matter-of-fact tone, "What are you up to today?"

And without pausing for an answer, he continued, "I just woke up and felt a prompting that I am supposed to do something with you today – so what is it?"

# Chapter Twelve: My Best Man

I wanted to keep secret what I planned to do that day. My calendar was clear at work. No meetings. No appointments. No need to tell anyone.

It was a month after my dream, the latter half of October 2009.

I realized my dream was a lot more than about Katie dying *SOON* – whatever *SOON* meant. I'll get into that further down on this page.

First, here are the plans I had for that day:

Get the kids ready for and off to school.

Wear my usual go-to-the-office clothes.

Instead of going to the office, go to the funeral parlors and cemeteries in town and look into buying a casket, cemetery plot, and take care of all these sorts of details. All the sorts of things that nobody wants to do or even talk about. But someone has to do them.

I also figured I would meet with the pastor to discuss memorial service arrangements.

You see, after a few weeks of feeling a general sense of relief due to the peace that the dream imparted to me, I began to realize that I had also been given actionable information. I realized that my dream was also a heads-up that I needed to get things in order now while I had some breathing room instead of possibly later when things got even more stressful.

This early warning was another way God helped me through this and helped me avoid additional frustration and last-moment stress. Even so, these were sad tasks that I never really was prepared to do. Yet I had decided that I was going to do them alone. Just knock them out quickly and get them behind me – like ripping off a Band-Aid – just get it done.

One thing that I kept wondering about was exactly what the angel in light had meant by the word *soon*. I had been told she would be leaving *soon*, but how do you define *soon* when it comes to a person's passing away?

Since it was a dream and the Spirit often uses spiritual vocabulary to communicate, I had attempted a Bible search to see if there were any references to the word *soon* to help me estimate how much time we were talking about.

First, before I continue the discussion about *soon*, I will brake for a very important observation I wish to share and it is another huge reason why we should read the Bible – a lot, over and over, forward and backwards. Because these are God's words, and God's language. He uses concepts and a lot of metaphors and especially uses a lot of visual images. He chose timeless images like those of a shepherd, a farmer, a tax collector, a fisherman, a judge, a woman getting water, a paralyzed man begging for help – these are powerful images that get past our intellect and into our hearts. He chose these examples so that His story and His ways would sink in deeper than our intellect – to the heart. He desperately desires us to search for Him and to find Him in His Word.

Understanding the Bible is like learning a foreign language. You start with the basics and it builds your vocabulary. As you continue you learn cultural insights and life lessons of that group of people. When you are at the higher levels of language understanding, you know enough to even tell jokes in their language and have probably developed the correct accent when you speak.

It is similar to learning about God – in a sense, the Bible is written in God's language. Or at least these are His words and concepts. So, the more you read His Word, the more you internalize His concepts and the more you will be able to recall them and apply them to your life – to real life.

His Word is never lacking and you will discover and grow your faith as you see for yourself the links between what He wrote centuries ago through God-inspired, chosen men, and what plays out in your life and in the world to this day.

Finally, when you are praying and want to understand something or understand a word or something the Lord has spoken to you directly, again, the first place to go is the Bible. I can't tell you how many times I simply look up a passage that contains a word or an idea I am given and –boom – there it is all spelled out in a specific sentence or an entire chapter. He is dropping hints or clues to direct you to precisely the place in scripture where you will get the full answer to what you are asking about, or gain a deeper spiritual understanding of what you need guidance about.

But, even though what I just described is very true most of the time, this time the word search wasn't very helpful. In the Book of Revelation it says, Behold I am coming quickly or soon – but that *soon* has been on the books for over 2,000 years and He still hasn't arrived for His second coming on earth.

What is *soon* to God could be a millennia to us or from our perspective. I didn't find any other scripture that seemed to be of much help. There is another passage that describes that the Lord is not slow as some consider slowness and I have learned that this is referring to the idea that God's movement in our lives often seems slow to us – because we want change or relief now – instantaneously – as in a miracle, but He often takes His own time and is not driven by man's schedule.

It has taught me a lot about patience. But I have also observed that God's timing is also often the perfect timing. He apparently knows of all sorts of other events that are all coming together and has things timed for the optimal results. Optimal in His larger plan, not necessarily optimal based on our immediate perspectives and desires. It is a delicate balance of trusting God to come through and waiting upon the Lord to come through at His optimal timing.

So often we take matters into our own hands and try to make something happen when we want to or when we think it ought to. That is the interesting dilemma we often find ourselves in – to wait upon the Lord or to take action. And when we take action – is it us striving for our desired result, or via a prompting from the Lord? That is the question we have to try to learn to pray about and learn to hear His sometimes still small voice to know the difference.

In any situation, regardless of whether we are to act or wait, I am certain of one thing – God desires us to ask. He desires us to seek His counsel. He desires us to be in relationship with Him the same way parents desire their grown children to still be in a relationship with them. Just because you are 18 or 22 and have moved out of the house, doesn't mean a parent is done offering good advice or life wisdom. In fact, it is probably then that the child is finally mature enough to ask insightful questions and strong enough to hear a true answer of wisdom.

It is the same with God. He has lots of wisdom to impart to us for our benefit, but He usually waits to be asked. You can go through your life just making random choices or relying on your own smarts, or you can pause, and humble yourself and turn to the inventor of wisdom and the One who sees the end from the beginning, and just ask. You will be richly rewarded.

This is not a salvation issue; it is plain smart living. It is also what God wants to use to bring you into greater alignment with His ways and with the way Christ lived. You can be more and more like Christ. The technical term is sanctification, but just think of it as emulating a really good mentor. You have only bad decisions to lose and untold blessings to gain.

Anyhow, back to my dilemma. I had tried simply looking up the word *soon* in scripture and felt I had no specific answer to what that should mean to me, now, in this situation. I also had tried praying about it and, as much as I wish I could always get a direct word from God, a simple text or paragraph or a short conversation, really that is extremely rare. It is often a small prompting at best, sometimes a word. This time I still had nothing more to go on.

Eventually, I reasoned that since the message was said to ME, and knowing that God is quite capable of tailoring a message to fit the understanding of the words that are spoken so that they would make sense to the person hearing them, I concluded that since there was no direct Bible interpretation for the term *soon*, that the person who could best determine what the word *soon* meant for this situation was – ME.

If the message was intended for me, God is smart enough to know what I would assume or be able to figure out what *soon* meant, so all I really needed to do was ask myself. And that is exactly what I did. I said to myself, "So, Eric – when you say *soon*, what do you mean?"

The answer is … it depends. If you mean are we leaving for lunch *soon?* – that could be anywhere between ten minutes to an hour. Clearly, that was not the case – it had already been four weeks and I had not sensed that her passing could possibly be any minute. But, if you asked me when are you going on an international vacation? – *soon* could mean anywhere between a month to almost a year.

I kept asking myself that question over and over and praying for discernment. As I narrowed down that word *soon* – my time span went from one month – one year, to two months – six months, to three to five months – and to finally – four months.

I had no way of knowing anything for certain, but somehow I settled on four months as a potential target timeframe. And, if that was the case, I was already just over a month into the four-month window. That little self-calculation seemed to confirm that I ought to get on with some of these uncomfortable tasks and not sit back and do nothing. I had preparations to make – like it or not and if I was smart and wanted to benefit from God's advanced warning, I had better get up off my butt and act now.

So my plan was to do this in secret. I made certain NOT to tell another soul what I was going to do. While I had gotten comfortable with the news, most other people were not able or ready to hear or accept that she was truly dying anytime in the near future. But, I felt I had it on good authority and should at least start this process.

But, going it alone?

God had other plans.

We never need to go it alone.

Just as I was ready to leave home, my cell phone rings and it is Jamie Bosworth, a good friend and leader of my men's Log House Bible study. After greeting him, I was shocked to hear him say in the most causal and matter-of-fact tone, "What are you up to today?"

And without pausing for an answer, he continued, "I just woke up and felt a prompting that I am supposed to do something with you today – so what is it?"

I sat in stunned silence for what felt like many pregnant pauses. The call shocked me. I did not want anyone else to know I was even starting to make such arrangements. Yet, I was struck by the uniqueness of this call. Jamie had NEVER before called to say something like that, and has never done it since. This was totally out of the blue and was a stunning coincidence. I almost felt called out by God. So I told him the truth and where I was heading.

He said to hold on and he would meet me at the first stop – the Mowell Funeral Home in town. I got there, he pulled up next to me in his white pick-up truck, and in we went – together. We sat through explanations of the services available and the fees, we toured a showroom of caskets – who knew there was a showroom for these things? I made some tentative choices and gave the necessary information.

For the rest of the day Jamie did the driving and I rode around with him in that white pick-up truck – visiting other funeral homes, and cemeteries, and finally stopping in at the church for a meeting with our pastor.

I share this little story because it illustrates a very powerful truth about God – He loves us very much and is looking out for our needs and for our heart. I had never thought to ask anyone to do something this hard with me, and had not given much thought or any prayer to the decision to spend the day doing this. It just seemed necessary and I planned to do it. I figured, I am the man here and this is what you do – you man-up and do the hard things – on your own.

But God had other plans. The truth is that we are never alone – God is always with us. And it is never God's desire that we do anything completely alone. He may send an earthly companion or a good friend, or even a stranger to be with us, and He, too, is also always with us. Sometimes we forget that, or don't feel His presence, but He is there and He wants us to NOT go it alone

This story shows the power and blessing of listening for that still small voice of God. Jamie listened and heard a prompting. He picked up the phone and did what may have felt a bit awkward, but he did follow that prompting. He was willing and listening and made himself available.

I can't tell you how much I appreciated that gesture from Jamie and from God. I should never have to do such things alone, and God saw to it that I didn't. That is the God we serve and love – the God who will never leave us or forsake us. O how He loves us – is a chorus from a praise song I once heard. It applies here – Oh how He loves us and brings us blessing upon blessing, even when we are walking through the valley of the shadow of death.

As it turned out, my method of estimating how soon *soon* actually was going to be was actually pretty accurate and supports my observation that when God talks to individuals, He uses words and meanings that will make sense to the individual. That is a very helpful thing to know. The actual day my wife passed was just under three months away, and I can say that when it did happen, it was immensely comforting to know these arrangements had been made, that God had provided me with adequate warning and a partner in Jamie to help so when the dreaded day arrived, things would be much easier.

The day after she passed, Jamie was with me as we went back to each of the places we had decided upon – the funeral home, the cemetery, and the church. It was like we had stepped through a dress rehearsal, so that when the real event was upon me, I had already rehearsed what needed to be done.

It may sound odd, but at the time I remember thinking that my friend Jamie was playing a role for me similar to the role the best man plays for the groom at a wedding. The best man's job is to make sure the groom has his stuff together – got the ring, got honeymoon tickets, got a ride to the church and other very practical things that the groom, who is caught up in the events of the day, is apt to forget.

Jamie was my best man for the occasion of my wife's passing. He will always have a special place in my heart for serving me in that way. In fact, when I remarried a year-and-a-half later, Jamie was the best man at my wedding.

## A footnote about Jamie

He is a pilot for Delta Airlines. Pilots don't always have control of their schedules. They have to put in for time off well in advance, and bid on what flights they will work. Jamie had no way of knowing when my wife would pass. He was slotted to fly a trip that day, possibly being out of the country for a few days.

When he got the news my wife had passed, he attempted to switch his schedule. But, it was to no avail. No one came forward willing to take his trip. He ended up going to Delta corporate headquarters and tried asking up the line if there was anything his supervisors could do to help him avoid the trip. He was again told no. But another pilot who *just happened* to be in the room overheard his request and why he desperately wanted the flight switch – so he could be there as my friend, and support and even serve as a pall bearer. The individual agreed to take the flight.

Jamie remains absolutely certain this was another God-thing. All his usual resources were not coming through, but God made a way and Jamie was present – walking me through a very hard thing, like my best man. I thank God for that rescue – again.

I was frozen in silence when Ann took me to the room prepared for the feast. Couldn't move or speak for seconds. Just stood in the threshold, beholding what was before me.

# Chapter Thirteen: Déjà Vu

Ever had an experience that made you feel like you had that experience before? They call it Déjà vu.

Thanksgiving 2009 was like that for me.

God set it up using Chick-fil-A staffer Ann Laramore. She was our department admin – a dear friend who shared a deep spiritual hunger for the Lord, like me. We talked about spiritual things together often, including things in our personal lives. Ann had been aware of a lot of my wife's developments, personal and spiritual, throughout the entire five-year cancer journey.

Another way God had blessed us for this time of struggle was simply my employment with Chick-fil-A. If you know the company for anything besides its great chicken, you probably know it is closed on Sunday. This is in keeping with the founder's practices and wishes that date back to the opening of his original restaurant in 1946.

Sunday was a family and worship day for the founder. He wanted employees to have the same opportunity.

It is a fantastic organization that is run on biblical principles. While there have been many blessings that have come to me over my 19 years on staff, I can say without a doubt that Chick-fil-A's finest hours for me were during this season of cancer struggles.

My supervisors were very supportive of me and my family, allowing me time to attend doctor appointments and take care of other chores as needed. When things were at their most stressful, they showered our family with food and even sent the corporate grounds crew to our home twice to cut the grass.

Other deeds stood out as absolutely over-the-top expressions of support. One was when Dan Cathy, the CEO and son of the founder, came to visit us in hospice. It was a place that he knew well because the Cathy family was a big supporter of the ministry, and had donated toward the building and grounds of the hospice. One evening, Dan came by himself to check on us and visit and spend time blessing us with his presence and caring. That one visit meant more than I can describe. Dan came and sat by our bedside, he shared words of comfort and inspiration. It was humbling that the CEO of the company knew of our situation, and prayed for us, and took time from his busy schedule to visit with us. There is just something powerful about the gift of presence – of time spent attending to others. With a company as large at Chick-fil-A, it is clear that Dan would have plenty of other people and matters requiring his attention – yet he chose to give his attention and his caring heart to us. It spoke volumes about who he is as a person and what the organization is about at its core.

Another highlight came months after her passing at the conclusion of a major equipment rollout project that I co-led during the months leading up to Katie's passing. At the end of such large projects, it would be customary to honor those who led the work with a special event or some kind of memento. What they did instead was present me with a large donation check made out to Southwest Christian Hospice in Katie's honor. That was another very powerful moment that I will forever remember and be humbled by.

There was one other massive expression of love and caring that came to me through Chick-fil-A. It was in the form of the help of another person – Ann Laramore.

As I said, she and I were already close friends and confidants, so when my supervisors thought about how best they could be of help, I think they realized that having the administrative and coordination efforts of someone like Ann would be very helpful. They allowed her to help me out during work time however she could.

She was always available to talk and advise. She helped make decisions and arrangements. We'd already shared a kindred spirit, talking about our personal lives and faith journeys. We took water cooler breaks, which at Chick-fil-A often meant ice cream cones and soda in our corporate café. We were prayer warriors for each other.

This took place in a variety of ways, but one of the most significant was helping plan an event for my family leading up to, during and after the Thanksgiving holiday. She was, quite simply, a God-send. Just as Jamie was a God-send, popping up when he did. God made sure I was not alone and that I had all the help I needed – and then some. God is a lavish giver and He did so through Ann and others.

It was early November – several weeks after my dream, and soon after the blessing of Jamie helping me. Thanksgiving was approaching and we had to decide how to handle that. Katie's family were spread out from New Jersey to Florida to California, and all were planning to come for what we all could sense may likely end up being the last gathering all around Katie to share as a family.

Rather than a very somber occasion, it turned into a positive, upbeat experience in the face of pending sorrow and death.

The idea of hosting these guests and planning and executing a Thanksgiving meal with our lives in such disarray focused on cancer treatments had seemed utterly daunting and insurmountable.

## A Thanksgiving to Remember

Ann pulled together an experience that was as well orchestrated as any high-level corporate event. She made all the calls and arranged for a fantastic Thanksgiving for our entire family.

She used her corporate contacts, got corporate rates, and arranged for lodging and a Thanksgiving feast in a private dining room in a nearby corporate-style conference center.

It was simply amazing.

Ann arranged for rooms and transportation from airports, and rented cars, and more.

We had a private dining room created in a meeting room space. Perfect accommodations – rooms in a very plush hotel facility with indoor swimming pools, and small-alcove gathering places.

Being Thanksgiving, we almost had the place to ourselves. Couldn't have been more perfect.

This was yet another time when I was reminded of Jesus' words to Paul:

"My grace is sufficient."

Everything was just what we needed. All the work of housing was taken care of. No need to burden our home that already was more like Grand Central Station. No need to shop or cook or entertain.

The feast was fit for a king.

Although Katie was exhausted, she was very appreciatively stunned by everything.

## I'd already been stunned speechless.

When Ann reviewed the preparations with me, we went over the menu, but I had not actually seen the room for the meal. I was already familiar with the facility from previous events, so I didn't feel the need to look at the actual space. I knew Ann would arrange for something very nice.

But, at the actual event, when I rounded a corner and stepped into the room, what I saw took my breath away.

I was frozen in silence and couldn't move or speak for several seconds. I just stood there in the threshold, beholding what was before me.

A room lavishly prepared for a banquet – fancy China, settings, and decorations. The walls on two sides were full glass floor to ceiling, with a bright view to well-kept grounds outside.

I knew I had seen a room quite like that before and I was remembering it vividly. That one room captured almost all of the elements of the three rooms I'd been shown in my dream. The brightly-lit room with two glass walls, and very fancy China and place settings, the table centerpieces – it felt so similar to that Heavenly place I had been taken to in the dream.

Throughout the meal I kept thinking of that dream and wondering if this was a fulfillment of it here on earth. It truly felt like a wedding rehearsal dinner.

Coincidence? Déjà vu?

Or not?

The next time I spoke to a nurse, she said, "It is time."
I told Katie. She simply said, "Are you sure?"

# Chapter Fourteen: The H Word

When people talk about cancer there are two words or topics that people seem to key into as they try to assess or grapple with the level of seriousness of the cancer.

People always seem to focus on the cancer stage. This is merely a number scale from 1 to 4 that is meant to describe the extent of the cancer growth.

They may not know much about cancer, but usually know that the higher the number the worse it must be, and a stage 4 is the worst and final stage. When they hear it is stage 4 they think this must be terminal and wonder how much time the patient has left to live.

The other topic people key on is the H word:

Hospice.

When they hear *hospice is* involved, they think the end is near. And it often is, though not always. You can have home hospice care for a long time, and sometimes patients recover or go into long remission even after hospice care is begun.

Anyhow, the common stereotype is there; otherwise, it would not be a stereotype.

When I had my dream, Katie's cancer had been stage 4 for some time.

We were in a gray period of just living with the disease, day-by-day managing symptoms. There was nothing more that modern medicine could do beyond pain and symptom management.

The cancer had spread to her lungs. She was on oxygen at home – tethered to this oxygen-generating machine that had a 50-foot-long hose that stretched from the living room to an upstairs bedroom. I learned to hate that machine. It droned on and on day and night. We found a small coat closet to tuck it into to muffle the noise, and in a way that would allow the oxygen hose to fit out the bottom of the closet door and reach upstairs to the bedroom and downstairs in the living room.

Still, this machine was a constant background soundtrack – one that I hated to hear. Part of my disdain for the machine was that it defined Katie's living radius – bedroom, bathroom, living room and kitchen. To go elsewhere, we had to connect to a portable tank that we had to pull around wherever we went. It was like being on house arrest.

We did the progressive steps at home, wanting to keep her surrounded by kids and family, and extended family and friends constantly visiting and giving their support.

Eventually we arranged for at-home hospice care. Nurses provided medical care several days a week. We relied on the nurses to tell us when it was time to transfer Katie to a hospice facility.

Not long after Thanksgiving – although still under 40 – she began to look like a frail, old woman. One night she was so thin, and her body ached so much she was only comfortable sitting in a chair with cushions for padding. She was not able to climb the stairs, even with my help.

I was in a quandary as to how to get her upstairs to the bedroom. I reasoned the only way I was going to safely get her upstairs was to lift her in the chair – but that would be a two-person job. Even though I had a number of friends to call on, it just felt really weird to ask anyone else to come over to help me lift my frail wife up the stairs.

So I turned to my son Matthew, an athletic 13-year-old, who loved baseball and was active in any sort of sport. I asked him to get the front legs of the chair while I grabbed the back legs. We carried his mom up the stairs together – him backing up the stairs; me walking forward.

Doing this simple task felt profound and horrible at the same time. We were taking her up the stairs one step at a time. I looked straight into Matthew's eyes. It felt to me like we shared a similar thought without saying a word.

It was just so sad and pathetic that we were having to carry her upstairs. A 13-year-old boy should not have to have this experience. It was a deep act of service but it was sad as well.

I didn't know it then, but God had another message in store for Matthew specifically, that would help strengthen his heart for this difficult time in his life. I will describe that in a chapter ahead.

It had sunk in to both of us just how bad things had gotten.

The next time I spoke to a nurse, she said, "It is time."

I told Katie. She simply said, "Are you sure?"

I nodded, "Yes."

Although we knew that day would come, it was heartbreaking. A lump formed in my throat as I watched Katie strapped to a stretcher that was lifted into the back of an ambulance, and the doors closed.

That news was – to me – a gift of confirmation from God – again – of Katie's presence in God's Country.

# Chapter Fifteen: Countdown To Departure
# Into God's Country

With Katie's transfer to a hospice facility, we knew her cancer-ravaged body would not last much longer. Her needs had become so intense that she needed that increased level of care.

We'd discussed the H word. We were highly blessed to learn about a nearby Christian ministry called Southwest Christian Hospice. They were a nonprofit, free-to-the-patient service providing both in-home and in-patient hospice care.

They were a God-send.

We'd agreed we did not want this to end at home. Sure, this was the place that not only Katie, but also I and our kids called home. Even though death is a natural experience – one that we all will go through – it just felt troubling to think she would die in our home.

I know others may feel differently about this. To me, it is different if you're talking about older persons living out their last days in their own homes. But my kids were now ages 10 and 13, and we presumably would continue living in that house.

It felt wrong to me that the house would have a death experience in it. I did not feel prepared to deal with that, along with everything else I was dealing with. The idea of waking up one day and walking into a room and finding her dead on my own was a troubling thought.

The way Katie asked, "Are you sure?" gave me great relief.

She was disappointed, and yet she was able to accept it with such peace and grace. She never got angry or kicked the dog or punched the wall or cried out in anger to God – not once. I was the one who'd act out and have to repent over and over.

Katie's attitude and spirit were amazing, and a huge inspiration to me and others.

Incredible – but true – from day one of hearing the C word applied to her, Katie's attitude was "Why not me? The rain falls on the just and the unjust. Why should I be immune to everything?"

What an amazing lady.

Hospice was good for Katie and our family.

The countdown to her transition on January 14, 2010 Into God's Country lasted six weeks.

The whole hospice staff were wonderful, true servants and gifted at what they did. Another wonderful friend was Chaplain Jim – Jim Weathers, one of the members of our Log House group that meets on Friday mornings. He had been a pastor most of his life so visiting us in hospice was a gift that came naturally to him and he gave that gift graciously. He visited often, sometimes when I was there and other times while I was off attending to other things. I did not learn of his chats with Katie about the angels in her room until over seven years later in late spring 2017.

That news was – to me – a gift of confirmation – again – of Katie's presence in God's Country.

The level of care the hospice staff provided was incredible. Physical needs. Emotional. Spiritual. They did it all. They allowed our friends to visit Katie. It was amazing to watch people come to visit her, faces burdened with worry and anxiousness. And then to see them a little later leaving with smiles and peace glowing on their faces.

It was hard to describe how a place associated with death was also so filled with life and light.

I think people came to pay their last visits and provide support to her and our family. But left being strangely filled with a positive sense, and were blessed and ministered to themselves.

I must share this as well. As things unfolded during this season, I kept sensing this sort of image of what was happening. I felt as if I were located in the middle of a giant tropical storm system – like what you see on the TV weather maps. The storm covers a very large area – often over multiple states. The winds in the center of the eye are calm, but the wind everywhere else is intense. The storm passes through an area and may leave a wake of destruction or simply leave its mark as it passes. If you are in the eye, things are calm, but everywhere else is being impacted.

This is the sense I had of how God was working. He had protected me and my family in the eye and had a swirl of others around me. And He was making an impact on everyone else around me – an impact on their hearts, and in the spiritual realm. The storm would not last forever – it would pass, but the landscape of people's hearts would change forever. I think He used our experience to impact many.

There were two special events which happened during that time. I will tell you about those in the Chapter: A Special Christmas.

With Katie in hospice, home life improved for me and the kids. We no longer lived constantly like we were in Grand Central Station, with people coming and going at seemingly all hours. We knew the care she was getting was much better than we could provide for her at home.

Much of the stress we'd had was lessened. That was another blessing from God.

God chose to answer my prayer in a way that was different and better than I could imagine. He spoke directly by the Spirit to Matthew's heart. It was an amazing moment we shared in the car in the rain in that Walmart parking lot.

# Chapter Sixteen: Matthew's Verse

At age 10 and 13, cancer was not a new thing to my daughter Kristen and son Matthew. They were 5 and 8 years old when the cancer journey began. Though we had tried to shield them from a lot of the long-term worries and concerns of a potentially fatal disease; still, they were alert and aware when things were not going well. Now their mom was in the hospice facility and the final outcome was getting quite clear.

I think my kids dealt with the crisis in different ways. Both were resilient and had a number of layers of support around them – from friends and teachers, to extended family members and church families who God had sent to surround us and provide whatever comfort they could. And they did provide comfort in innumerable ways that could fill an entire book.

But, being three years older, I think Matthew was old enough to grasp the gravity of the situation more and was more affected by it. They had watched their mom deteriorate right before their eyes – and it was a hurt that recurred daily, like what prisoners in an enemy prison must feel like when they wake and go about their day. No matter what happens, they are trapped in a prison.

Cancer in its darkest stages can feel a lot like that.

On one hand, throughout the entire cancer experience, I had prayed that regardless of the outcome that she would not suffer. And by suffer I meant the kind of relentless pain that is true suffering. Now, she did suffer in many ways – in the suffering of this abrupt and terrible change in her life, and in the loss of all her previous hopes and dreams, her intensions to be a mom and raise her kids up to adulthood. But, on the other hand, she never did suffer from a lot of actual physical pain. It was suffering to watch it, but God did honor that prayer to avoid the brutal type of suffering.

In any case, despite telling my kids about my dream experience and doing my best to describe what I experienced, I always wondered just how much I was able to really pass along. Again, how do you pass along an experience of a surgical healing on the

inside? I just had to pray that God's grace would be sufficient –
and it was.

## Rainy day in a Wal-Mart parking lot

On one particular day when I had what seemed like a
thousand errands to run, Matthew was with me. As we parked at a
Wal-Mart, the sky opened up and rained hard for some time.
Rather than get drenched, I took the time to sit with Matthew in the
car and just talk. It seemed we were always too busy tending to
things that it was actually hard to find white space to just talk. I
asked him how he was doing and we talked about spiritual matters.
I recapped for him some of the powerful words of healing that I
had received from my dream when Matthew told me that he had
received a verse from God as well.

I was surprised – I had not heard anything about this.

He went on to explain that actually he had been feeling down
for some time, and was starting to feel bad and left out wondering
why other people who were not very close to his mom were getting
dreams and visions that brought comfort and assurance but he had
not received any.

He continued, explaining that one day while simply walking
up the stairs in our house, he just heard a voice call out –
completely out of the blue. He said it wasn't an audible voice, but
more like a voice speaking inside his head. The voice said simply
John 16:22.

Matthew continued immediately up to his room and looked up
that passage in his Bible and could not believe how accurate and
timely hearing a reference to that passage was for him. The verse
read:

"So, with you: Now is your time of grief, but I will see you
again and you will rejoice, and no one will take away your joy."

He instantly knew what that word for him meant – that it is ok
to grieve – this is a time to be grieving. But you will see your
mom again and you will rejoice at that time. And when you do, no

one will take away your joy. In other words, when you see her again, you will be filled with joy and it will be in the Kingdom of Heaven, because you will never have that joy taken away again. You will be reunited with your mother and will never experience the pain of loss or separation again – for all of eternity.

Now that was a message of hope. That is the entire Christian message of resurrection.

When he told me, I was filled with joy as well. Not only for this truth, but because the Lord had revealed it to Matthew. I kept wondering if my story would be enough and wondering what else I could say to help nurture his heart over this huge loss. I never asked God for this gift – I only prayed and lifted up my concerns to Him – concerns about how to reach my children's hearts and give them the full measure of comfort that I had received.

God chose to answer my prayer in a way that was different and better than I could imagine. He spoke directly by the Spirit to Matthew's heart. It was an amazing moment we shared in the car in the rain in that Walmart parking lot.

## John Chapter Sixteen

When I went home later, I researched the passage and was fascinated and even more comforted by it as I read more of the context around it.

The entire chapter of John 16 is very powerful. It is where Jesus warns His disciples of trials that will come, but in the same breath comforts them by explaining that though He will be leaving them soon, they cannot truly ever lose Him or His presence.

He is trying to encourage them so that they will not fall away. He tells them that He is going back to God the Father, who sent Him. He acknowledges their grief, but then goes on to say that it is good that He is going away. He tries to explain that after He leaves, He will send the Comforter (the Holy Spirit) to come to them. He goes on to say He has much more to say to them – more than they can now bear.

But then He says something very profound in John 16:13 instructing them that, "... when He, the Spirit of truth, comes, He will guide you into all the truth. He will not speak on His own; He will speak only what He hears, and He will tell you what is yet to come.

[14] He will glorify Me because it is from Me that He will receive what He will make known to you.

[15] All that belongs to the Father is Mine. That is why I said the Spirit will receive from Me what He will make known to you."

This is a powerful passage for many reasons.

What Jesus is trying to convey is that while He will be leaving the earth, no longer present in the bodily form that they had come to know Him, He would be sending His Spirit which will speak many more things to them and to all Believers. When the Spirit speaks, it will be God's truth and Jesus' truth.

This is the concept of the triune God – three and one – separate but united as well. Therefore, the disciples and none of the future children of God will ever truly be without Jesus – He said the Spirit would receive from Jesus what God wants to make known to you. The Spirit will only speak what He hears God the Father and/or Jesus pass along.

He is also saying that the Spirit will tell you things that are yet to come.

This means He will be speaking either truths about the world and Heaven or truths about your particular life – truths straight from God. This was true of Matthew's passage and of my dream and of all the dreams and visions that were revealed. This was God Himself speaking to His children – telling us what was to come. He points out that the Spirit will glorify Jesus because it is from Jesus that these words of truth come from or through.

And then, we get to the specific passage that Matthew was given by the Spirit. It goes on to say in verse 20:

"You will grieve, but your grief will turn to joy.

[21] A woman giving birth to a child has pain because her time has come; but when her baby is born she forgets the anguish because of her joy that a child is born into the world.

[22] So with you: Now is your time of grief, but I will see you again and you will rejoice, and no one will take away your joy.

How absolutely powerful a passage – it talks of a season of grief that must come, in the same way that a woman must go through a period of pain just before there is a birth unto a new life. Likewise, when a loved one dies, there is a season of grief that must come, but for those who believe in Christ, this grief gives way to a great joy because of a birth into a new life.

Believers in Christ, who do actually die their earthly death, don't die, but instead simply pass through the process that leads to new life. The new life in Heaven that cannot be taken away. This is the everlasting joy, the joy that is the good news that Christ has overcome the horrible power of death. This chapter of scripture ends with this verse:

[33] "I have told you these things, so that in Me you may have peace. In this world you will have trouble. But take heart! I have overcome the world."

What a powerful, comforting declaration of hope and joy.

This is Jesus assuring us that He is sharing all this so that we may have peace –true peace – like that peace that passes all understanding. Then He affirms what we all know too well to be true – that in this world you WILL have trouble – no kidding. This life can seem like an almost endless stream of trouble at various seasons of life. Man is born to trouble, as the sparks fly up to Heaven it says elsewhere.

But He ends with the most powerful statement of all: He tells us to take heart – be encouraged and joy-filled.

Why?

Because He has overcome the world. He has already overcome everything and anything that the world can throw at us – including our own physical death. Nothing can take away His power over death and His assurance to be by our side at that moment to resurrect and restore and transition us into His Kingdom.

The dreams and visions that were revealed – they are to give us peace and comfort, to give God glory for His great gift of life and to assure us and show us what that restoration to new life actually looks like.

This is the bottom line of Christianity:

God loves us and wants to share His love with us, for eternity, if we will humble ourselves and choose to be His sons and daughters by making Him Lord of our life. He doesn't force Himself on us, but He simply states, "Behold, I set before you blessings and curses, death and life ... choose life that you may live with Me forever."

One last thought:

When Matthew shared this it was a huge joy to find out that he too had heard from the Lord in a very specific and powerful way.

I was also pleased because I think it helped me get across another concept that I wanted him to understand clearly – that while so much of these dream experiences seemed to center around his mom and how she would be ok and how she would be restored and brought up into Heaven, there was another very important point:

God was also with us back down here on earth where we still are subject to all sorts of trials and troubles. He had not abandoned us. In fact all these messages from the Spirit are proof that He loves us all so dearly and is never far from us.

I wanted Matthew and Kristen to know in no uncertain terms that we were not going to despair; that we were moving forward with our lives in confidence. God had shown up and was with us in all times and in all situations. We were not giving way to fear or sorrow – but moving forward in life with a stronger than ever sense of God's abundant life.

And you know what?

That's just what we did.

God had rescued the hearts of all of us.

When it passed, I looked down at the page and I had somehow written two letters in each circle, and the circles were intersecting and formed a triangle. In one circle was written ES, in another RH and in the third, UK. I had no idea what that was about or what to make of it.

# Chapter Seventeen: Kristen's Faith

Children often can be beacons of faith. A good example is my daughter Kristen when she was still only 10 years old. It happened a bit after her mom's passing into God's Country. But the roots of what was to develop began spreading while my wife battled cancer.

One of the things my wife did to keep in contact with everyone was to give updates on a web site called CaringBridge. It is a website specifically for cancer patients where information is easy to share with others, and people can, in turn, read and post their positive comments of love and encouragement for the family members.

It can become a sort of log of a person's cancer journey. Katie was a frequent user and updater on this site. It helped tremendously with the burden of keeping others informed and was a huge blessing.

As she became more bedridden, a friend gave us a laptop computer. I didn't realize it at the time that a classic example of God working in the details was unfolding.

I started it up and began setting it up on our Internet service so she could use it. To test out the Internet search, I decided to surf over to check out the website of Ransomed Heart Ministries run by John Eldredge. They promote all his books and other resources.

The ministry also puts on live events – most for men only, and a few for women only led by his wife Staci Eldredge. As I described earlier, God used the works of John Eldredge to teach and minister to me in powerful ways through the entire five-year journey through cancer. Remember, it was John's most popular book, *Wild at Heart,* that we used in that men's Bible study group that kicked off immediately before the first diagnosis.

Before that I was not a reader of his or a fan. But something just clicked with that first book and that group of Log House men. These guys ended up being great prayer warriors for me in those first and hardest days.

And God just took off from there. My hunger for Him and my delight at how John teaches grew as I devoured book after book. *Wild at Heart* is John's most popular book, I guess because it resonates with the hearts of most men.

But I came to discover that it might not be the best of his works. Truly he is like a modern day C.S. Lewis. His other books, including *EPIC, The Sacred Romance, Journey of Desire, Waking the Dead, Fathered by God, Walking with God, Beautiful Outlaw* and so many others, are all amazing works, powerful disclosures of just who God is and how He works.

My heart was – and remains – so strengthened by these works that are still being written by John.

If this sounds like an infomercial about Eldredge and his ministry – it is. I cannot not share what God used as a very powerful teacher for me in this season of trial and growth.

## Eldredge events can be difficult to attend.

Typically, Eldredge live events, called Boot Camps (as opposed to retreats) are held two or three times a year and usually far off in Colorado. The events are so popular that you have to submit to get into a lottery just to have a chance to be able to purchase a ticket to attend.

The way the lottery works, you have to be aware and watch out for the event and the open dates for submitting a request to the lottery in advance. Then when the lottery window is open, you have to be certain to log in during that period and submit an application. If there are not enough slots, you will get an email saying they are sorry but hopefully a slot will be available at the next event.

And you attempt this whole process again later in the year.

But if you don't make the lottery to get a slot, they often give you some sort of code that you can use when signing up for the next ticket lottery. That code usually is enough to make it likely you will get a spot on your next try.

Over the previous five years, I had gone to see John and experience the Boot Camps two times in person – both were very powerful events where the focus turns out to encounter God rather than flock to an earthly author. I had also become a bit of a practitioner of such events as well, leading class after class in my church teaching from his books and helping to lead similar boot camps for men locally in the North Georgia Mountains. I just couldn't get enough.

Anyhow, on that evening when I was testing out the computer, just for a place to search to, I went to the Ransomed Heart website. And I felt an urge to click on the *events* page. I don't know what prompted me to click there – I just did it without thinking, really. I scanned down to see what might be in the works and was surprised to see that they were having their first event in Europe – hosting a retreat for men in the UK.

I remember looking at the event, and even though it was many months away, I noticed that I had just happened to be checking during the narrow window of time that the lottery was open to even attempt to get a ticket to that event.

For a moment, my heart jumped and I thought I would love to go to that event. But, my reality came crashing back in another instant. What was I even thinking? We were in what was clearly a difficult time. My wife's cancer was back and could be serious for who knows how long. There was no way I should even be thinking about attending something like this, especially something so far away – on another continent. It was simply out of the question.

This was about a month before I had my dream and before the symptoms started to clearly go downhill.

I clicked away from the page. But, as I was putting the computer away, suddenly a memory came back to me with crystal clarity. On one previous Ransomed Heart retreat, during one of the many times we were sent off in silence after a talk to just spend time listening and journaling with God, I had prayed and was writing in my journal quite a bit that seemed to flow from my fingers about some questions I had posed to the Lord. I was still very new to praying and listening, journaling, and hearing any sort of answer.

And this is the odd thing that happened. For whatever reason on the last page of my journal, I drew three circles that intersected, like the image of the Trinity. And then I started writing letters in each circle. I didn't remember consciously writing this, the letters just seemed to come through my hand. It was quite odd and only lasted a moment or two. When it passed, I looked down at the page and I had somehow written two letters in each circle, and the circles were intersecting and formed a triangle. In one circle was written ES, in another RH and in the third, UK. I had no idea what that was about or what to make of it. It was my last journal entry and I gave it little additional thought. It almost seemed like a doodle – though I am not one who ever doodles in the margins.

Fast forward over a year or two to the night I was testing out this new computer. As I was putting it away, I could distinctly see that image of the page in my prayer journal with those three circles. I jumped up and found that journal to look at it again. Sure enough, there were the three circles and initials. Suddenly the meaning seemed to be apparent:

ES is my initials. RH is Ransomed Heart. UK is the United Kingdom.

I thought, "What ... no, that can't be ... this doesn't make sense – I can't even be thinking of such a thing now – there is no way I can go or should go."

But, in a strange sense of obedience, I went back on the website and filled out the lottery request. I also figured, this is for Europeans; they probably don't want any Americans to fill up the slots anyway, and what I should expect is to get the typical rejection letter with the code to use on some future event. This is what my commonsense told me – there is no way I am going to the UK – period.

I sent off the email and waited. And you know what? I was right – I got the exact form letter I was expecting, telling me that the event was already full, but I had a code good for a future event. I thought, "Well, good. That is settled. I don't need to think about any trip to the UK."

Then everything I have described in this book took place – my dream, her passing, the dreams and visions of the others – massive life change. Thoughts of this event were the furthest thing from my mind.

Once evening not long after my wife had passed, my daughter Kristen and I were out walking the dog, Cody. I could write a chapter just talking about this dog and what a God-send he was. He was a brown Labrador Retriever who neither retrieved nor did much of anything you would expect from a hunting dog breed – like he hated water or going outside to even get his paws wet in the rain.

But he was really good at one thing:

He was an indoor dog who loved to follow you around and sit in your lap or next to you or at your feet. He was the *PERFECT* companion dog for someone going through cancer. He stayed by Katie's side through thick and thin and was a source of comfort to both my kids and me. I loved that dog.

## Kristen had the perfect comeback.

Anyway, we were walking the dog and just talking about life and stuff and my phone vibrated in my pocket, indicating an email. I pulled my phone out and saw an email from Ransomed Heart. I passed the leash to Kristen as I checked the email.

It said, "Congratulations."

I had been granted an opportunity to attend John Eldredge's boot camp event in the UK. I was stunned and said almost under my breath, not realizing I was even speaking out loud, "Wow – God does answer prayers."

Kristen said, "Well, of course He does, Dad."

I was stunned again. I hadn't realized I said that out loud so that she could hear. So I told her of the news and she shared her surprise and joy with me. Once again God had been quietly working in the details, this time making sure I'd be in the UK for this event, which would turn out to be a blessing for more than just me.

I loved that my daughter, who had just gone through this difficult loss of her mom, still instinctively and instantly believed that God answers prayers, and said out loud that, "Well, of course, He does …"

It was such a joy to know her faith was so strong. Out of the mouths of babes …

## God sent me to the UK to give encouragement.

I knew God was letting or sending me to this event to restore my heart after a long season of trial and duty. He knew I would love nothing better than to get to go on such an adventure, and it was glorious – fantastic. But I was also wondering why else I was there. The content was essentially what I had seen and received before. In fact, I had taught this material myself to other men. It is always helpful to get exposed to great teachings a second time, but I knew there was something more – but what?

It may be one or both of these things:

At these events, John and his ministry staff make themselves very scarce after the sessions. They don't want the event to be about them or about connecting with their readers or fans. It is about creating an environment for the individuals who attend to connect with God. That is the purpose. So they usually make themselves hard to find, to allow the men to spend time with God.

But on the last day, after the last session, John usually is available, and often takes hours talking to the men who line up to say a few words and perhaps get him to autograph a book or two. I stood in the line at that event and I can only say it was a holy moment and a distinct honor to get to say a few words to him, face to face.

In just a few sentences, if you can imagine me being brief, I told him my basic story – about the cancer and about when I first started reading his works and how over the years and during that season how much God had used him and his words to nurture and mature and grow my heart. And when I told him of my wife's recent passing I was able to say to him, "John, the man you see here today, who got through this so well with God's help, is not the same man you would have met five years ago – before all of this and before I read your books. God used you to reach me and my heart and I am forever grateful."

We shared a moment. He is a modest man, never wanting to draw attention to himself. I must assume that God had this as a purpose of my being there. I was there to give him a simple pat on the back, or perhaps to deliver a much needed sign or message of encouragement that his works and his heart for God mattered and was bearing tremendous fruit in the Kingdom.

Finally, there may have been another reason I was there that I may never get confirmation on till I reach God's Country. As I said, John and his staff become scarce at these events, but I was a longtime fan and reader and I knew the other presenters and key ministry speakers as well.

By what felt at the time like chance, I was able to grab a seat at lunch one day with one of those other men – Craig McConnell. He was a really amazing guy as well – a gentle man with great wit and humor, self-deprecating in his talks to make a point and be real and transparent. I sat next to him and over what turned out to be a fairly long lunch, I told him my story. An extended version of what I later said to John.

I wanted Craig to also know the deeply powerful work that his words and this ministry had been to me. Now, Craig was a gentle guy, but when you got close to him, you realized he was also quite a big guy. I guess the video takes off some weight and height for some people. Perhaps I have a hope in video. Anyhow, up close and in person, he was like a big gentle bear. And as I spoke, I could see he was getting choked up and eventually unable to hold back some tears.

I was a little surprised. I really did not think my story would have that kind of effect. Again, I thought that perhaps this was another reason why I was there – to help speak to Craig's heart and minister to him and give him some much-needed words of affirmation or something like that. He seemed deeply touched – perhaps more than I realized at the time. We often don't know at the time the impact our words may have on others – but God does and He knows how to position us to pass along what He wants passed along and give words of encouragement and comfort to others.

Overall, I had an amazing trip, visiting the castles and cathedrals of the UK and returned home a week later. In addition to attending this milestone event, God had arranged for me to visit the entire time with a family that was on mission in the UK. They hosted me and we had a tremendous time visiting the sights of that splendid country. It was an incredible God-send of a trip that I was certain God had used for various reasons and I was content to wait and see if some other reasons would become apparent after I returned home.

I have since sensed that there was more to it for Craig. In the months that followed, it came out on the Ransomed Heart website that Craig had a rare form of cancer in his blood. When I heard more details, I was able to pretty well figure out that he must have known of the diagnosis and was perhaps even under some form of treatment when he was at that event and when we shared that lunch together.

I cannot know for certain, but I rather suspect that somehow God was delivering a message of hope to Craig through me. I believe he was somehow comforted and strengthened as iron sharpens iron.

It was an honor to be able to thank John and Craig in person and perhaps share words of strength and comfort to another who is walking through his own cancer journey. Craig transitioned into God's Country in 2016. His spiritual strength came through during that period as he continued to provide very moving and powerful insights in their weekly podcasts. He was a friend and inspiration to many, a well-loved servant and friend of God.

On the day of the interment, they had a small service at the graveside. A huge rainbow stretched across the sky from one horizon to another.

# Chapter Eighteen: God Cares About The Unborn

Sometimes I've felt like a human magnet that attracts amazing accounts from people who've had awe-inspiring encounters with God-sent messengers. Here is such an encounter. It is about an unborn baby. The story was told to Katie and me while we were in the midst of our six-week experience at SW Christian Hospice. Between Thanksgiving and Christmas 2009.

It's worth inclusion in this book. I believe it will lift the spirits of any mom who has had such an experience; also, parents of babies and children under the age of accountability who've died. They are special to God, and will live eternally in God's Country.

Here it is:

I was contacted by a friend and former church member, Mike Bodger. A few years previous he had felt led by God to leave his successful secular sales job and enter seminary to go into formal pastoral training.

He and his family were members of my church. I remember helping him pack up his house after he had quit his job, sold his house, and was moving his wife Elaine and family into grad student housing at a seminary nearby in Atlanta.

I lost close touch with him, though we got updates on his educational progress from time to time. Upon his graduation just a few months before our conversation he had completed his degree and accepted his first call to serve as a pastor at a church in Florida.

He and Elaine were still probably getting used to the new community and their new roles when they heard word about Katie being in hospice. Mike reached out and I happened to be visiting at the hospice when the call came in. I had stepped out to the prayer garden to take the call. We had quite a long conversation as I brought Mike up to speed and told him about my dream.

As I wrapped up my story, Mike said what I have heard a handful of other people say – that he too had a fantastic story to share. But he did not want to share this over the phone. He insisted that he and Elaine would spend a day to travel up and visit with us at Katie's bedside to tell us their story in person. We made plans for them to visit later that week.

Remember, another thing that made this sudden visit all the more remarkable was that we came from a Presbyterian background and he was an ordained minister in the Presbyterian Church.

This kind of talk, as I said in the beginning of this book, was just not something that gets talked about in that denomination – at all, ever. Likewise in most other mainline denominations. So this was all the more unique to me that a pastor was willing to listen and accept my dream story and then go on to share a similar story with me.

## Their story

When they arrived, I brought them into the room and set up chairs so the three of us could sit around Katie's bed and she and I could hear this fantastic story that they were so eager to share in person.

As they began telling some background to their story, the foggy details of an incident in their past started to come back into focus. Elaine had been pregnant and carried the baby to almost full term when she suffered an unexpected miscarriage on Christmas Eve two years previous.

It was while they were in seminary, and I remembered bits of stories about other people from our church ministering to them when they heard of this tragic news at such a difficult time of the year. Not that suffering a miscarriage has any better seasons or worse seasons, but forevermore they would certainly think of the child they lost at every Christmas that would come in the future. It is a shame when something so tragic gets associated with something that previously had only positive associations. That is one of the hardships of sudden loss tied to a specific time or place. It can almost make the season haunted or depressive, and it can rob our joy for years or even a lifetime to come, especially if the grief is unresolved and unhealed.

As Mike and Elaine reminded us of the details, they started telling us things we did not know and had never heard before. He described how difficult the passing of their child was and how traumatized it left them, especially Elaine.

She nodded her agreement to everything Mike was sharing.

He described her as devastated. It was as if all the life had left her spirit as well. She was barely functional in her grief, as a wife and as a mother to their first-born child. The shock and the dismay and the loss was just too traumatic for her to just keep going. This baby had been tended to so carefully and was at full term – planned to be delivered within a week.

To make matters worse, after the miscarriage, the doctors discovered some sort of hereditary medical condition that Elaine had that, if they had known this in advance or had tested her to discover this condition, they could have exercised greater care and could have delivered the baby just a bit early and both baby and mother would in all likelihood have been fine.

Discovering this after the fact didn't change what happened, but knowing that a simple precautionary step that could have been done if this had been known in advance just made it all the worse.

As a man, I have no way to fully appreciate how devastating this is for a woman to lose a baby. Mike was doing as good a job as he could to describe just how taken out his wife was, lost in depression and despair, that lasted for many weeks after that incident. She remained that way, day after day until God showed up in a supernatural way – she also had a powerful dream that changed everything.

## A Heavenly place in the clouds

Elaine picked up the story from there. One night, while in deep sleep, she described being transported in a dream up to what she described as a Heavenly place in the clouds. She found herself standing next to an angel clothed in white whose face was shining like the sun. It was a warm and happy place and they stood by a wall or bench.

Then the air was filled with the sounds of children's laughter. As she looked around about them, there were children of all ages and sizes running around laughing and playing in a beautiful field of green grass. It was like sitting in the middle of a school playground at recess. There was a lot of general noise of happy children and as they sat there – the angel in white remaining silent – suddenly one voice in particular could be heard clearly talking to her.

It cut through and on top of the din of the other children's laughing and shouting. The voice said to her, "Mom, it's me, Matthew Noel. I'm here in Heaven and everything is fantastic."

As she heard this voice, she instantly recognized or was made to know and recognize this as the voice of the unborn child she had lost. She began frantically looking around her, at all these kids, trying to pick out the one that had said this to her.

Remember, this child had never been born and she only knew the sight of a stillborn baby, not the appearance of a grown child let alone ever heard it make a sound, much less speak. Yet there was no denying what she knew to be true. Her child had spoken to her – if she could only pick him out in the crowd so she could reach out and embrace him. But, try as she might, she could not identify which child had spoken this to her.

Then, to her surprise because she had almost forgotten the angel in white who was right next to her, the angel turned to her and spoke some profound words of comfort. She was told the following:

1. "I will never again take away one of your little ones."
2. "You must trust and wait for the blessing."
3. "Look to the sign of the rainbow."

That was it. Dream over.

Then Mike picked up the story. He said the next day his wife told him about the dream, after which she immediately was another person. Gone was the mother overrun with grief and sorrow, gone were the tears and depression that had invaded and taken root in her heart. She was fully alive again, back among the land of the living, as it were. She was her old self again, happy to be alive and with her family and raising their first child, Nathaniel.

Mike kept stressing the immediate relief, the change, the restoration that she experienced after this encounter. As he spoke, I knew exactly what he meant – it was how I had felt immediately after my dream. When the Lord touches and heals your heart, you feel like a whole new person.

## More to their story

They continued, as a lot had happened since then until now.

Mike told how not long after that, they discovered Elaine was pregnant again. And this time, the doctors knew of her medical condition and they were all unanimous in giving her their medical opinion that she should not consider herself as pregnant – in her condition, this would almost certainly not result in a viable fetus or a live birth.

They were just giving her their best medical opinion so she would not get her hopes up again. They had told her that she needed to accept the fact that she was really never going to be able to conceive again and, frankly, it would be too risky anyway.

But, while the men in white jackets told her one thing, she remembered the words – no, the promise – that a man in a white robe had told her in a dream:

**"I will never again take away one of your little ones."**

She chose to wait and trust in the words she had received. She waited the full term of her pregnancy and you know what?

She gave birth to a healthy baby boy whom they named John. And two years later, they gave birth to another son named Peter.

This story is a great hope for anyone who has lost a child either before birth or anywhere below the age of accountability. We now have nearly eye-witness proof that God rescues and restores even the unborn children. She was not permitted to see and identify her child, but certainly will when she enters into and becomes a permanent resident in God's Country: Heaven.

In the meantime, she was given a glimpse behind the veil that divides this world and Heaven. She was given a view of God's ways and His heart toward all His children, including her unborn child and her and her family.

God has this all in His hands. Not a sparrow nor an unborn baby falls to the ground without His knowledge and His intervention. Children are apparently in a special category – they seem to get a *get into Heaven free card*. Oh how we all may wish for such a pass. We don't get such a pass once we live past the age of accountability, where the Lord will then hold each person accountable for our own decision whether or not to trust and believe and confess our faith in the Lord.

## A follow-up confirmation

At the time they had that miscarriage, they had the body cremated and kept the ashes in an urn awaiting the proper opportunity to bury it closer to their family plot that was much further away. You see, they were people who had emigrated to the U.S. from the UK and they still had family back in the UK.

In the months after the dream experience, something happened with their travel visas and suddenly they got word that they had a very short time to return to the UK to renew their travel documents that enabled them to return and reside in the U.S. When they hastily made travel arrangements, they contacted her mother and asked her to line up a suitable burial plot for them to have a small graveside interment while they were in the UK on this trip.

On the day of the interment, they held a small service at the graveside for their child that had passed away, Matthew Noel. And guess what happened on that day ... a huge rainbow stretched across the sky from one horizon to another. The last of the three words from the Lord was fulfilled.

Not only was this a specific sign that she was told to watch for, but the rainbow has always been a sign God has used in the heavens dating back to its use after the flood had wiped out all life on the earth, except for Noah and his family and all the animals he had collected in the ark. The rainbow is a sign of God's covenant to protect His children and never again take them out by an act of flood.

## One last footnote

Before they left our community to take their first calling at a church in Florida, their family helped paint a mural on the wall in the children's Sunday School wing of the church. It depicted Jesus, sitting among children, with the passage from scripture where He instructs his disciples to let the children come unto Him and do not deny them. Painted in the background, streaming across the painted sky is a huge rainbow. They deliberately put the rainbow in that picture, and now you know why.

## The takeaway

Elaine's dream speaks volumes about the fate of the unborn. It also speaks the truth that a fetus is a life and has a soul. I shared their story because these questions, about what happens to children is a common question and miscarriages are a lot more common than people often realize. It should be a great comfort that God extends the offer of eternal life to everyone, and to those who pass away before they are ever witnessed to, or even after they are witnessed to, but are not old enough to make a conscious, rational and informed decision for or against Christ. This also should give great comfort to those who have family members who are mentally impaired. God is kind and merciful and extends His grace to all who do not choose against Him. If one is unable to make a choice for God, He does not seem to hold that against them. In fact, it appears they get the most valuable pass into eternal life of all. When a child is lost, it is painful for those who survive, but take heart, God has overcome death itself and they are alive and well, fully healed and fully alive and living in the presence of the Lord.

What really makes me wonder who the messenger was that spoke in the dream to Elaine, was the promise:

"I will never again take away one of your little ones."

# Chapter Nineteen: One In Ten

Telling Mike Bodger about my dream, and hearing his and wife Elaine's story in return, brought to mind an interesting statistic.

I've noticed as I have shared my dream over and over, about 10% of the time, the people I am sharing with have a similar kind of personal dream or vision encounter story to share with me.

Mind you, I am not talking about the general public, like in a national poll. I usually share my story with what I would describe as a fairly similar population of committed Christians, and within that group, yes – I have heard a number of amazing stories from about one in ten people.

The common themes seem to be that in each case, the person who received the vision or had an encounter was always in the midst of something quite stressful or traumatic. And in each case, the vision or message was often delivered by an angelic being who is clothed in white.

The message has always been a very positive, comforting message that is highly specific to that person's life and situation.

It is often when a person is wracked with internal struggles or turmoil about something difficult that is happening, that the God of all comfort sends an angel or a messenger, or perhaps it is the Lord Himself appearing.

One school of thought is that when angels appear, they routinely introduce themselves so there is no chance of confusing them with the Lord. They in no way want to inspire worship of themselves; but rather, to direct worship to the true and living God who sent them to bring some important news.

In my case and in some other cases; for example, Elaine's experience, when the being clothed in white whose face shines like the sun does not introduce himself or herself, I have come to believe that there is a good chance it could be the Lord Himself.

In my dream, I kept asking over and over, "Who are you?"

And I never was told an answer. Perhaps this is because the Lord should need no introduction. He may have been thinking,

"You know who I am" and chose not to answer the obvious. Still, it was so stunning to me at the time, I could not help but voice my astonishment and ask, "Who are you that at the sound of your voice you can deliver such healing and comfort?" Upon reflection later, I thought of the words the disciples said when they observed and experienced Jesus as He calmed the storm. They marveled saying, "Who is this man that even the wind and the waves obey Him?" I think they were simply saying out loud what was astonishing them on the inside and their question in some ways begs the obvious answer. This must be the Lord of Heaven who has power like this to calm the storms of life.

I may have to wait till I cross into God's Country to get final confirmation, but to this day I am not certain whether my encounter was from an angel sent to me from the Lord or was the Lord Jesus Himself. All I do know is that it certainly was from God and had plenty of hallmarks of His presence. I tend to now think it was the Lord Jesus Himself.

What really makes me wonder who the messenger was that spoke in the dream to Elaine, was the promise:

"I will never again take away one of your little ones."

Again, I think it could very well have been the Lord, since He also did not introduce Himself and He, alone, holds the keys to life and death. So it would follow that only the Lord can make a statement like that to her.

During all that she suffered through, Katie always kept a positive attitude. It was not a mask. It was real. The kind of deep, positive outlook that only comes from a spiritual anchoring in the Lord.

# Chapter Twenty: A Special Christmas

My kids and I anticipated spending Christmas in the hospice, along with immediate family, crammed around a hospital bed in a cramped room with a TV.

A room surrounded by seven other rooms, each with a cancer patient in the final stages of death – not exactly what you want or eagerly look forward to, especially at Christmas.

But God intervened, yet again.

Katie rebounded and began to gain strength. In the days leading up to Christmas the hospice nurses hinted that maybe they could arrange for her to go home for Christmas.

It sounded like a pipe dream, but as the days marched on, so did her recovery.

On December 24 they said they'd release Katie to our home for 24 hours.

It was a huge blessing for her and for us.

We watched Christmas videos, and a church service on a big screen in the living room. We read the Christmas nativity story and did some other Christmas Eve traditions.

Katie slept next to the Christmas tree on the living room couch. It was very touching and a powerful blessing – a special Christmas gift from the Lord.

She enjoyed a wonderful Christmas Day meal. Her eyes were moist – not from sorrow – but from joy from getting to be with family in her own home one more time.

The respite from hospice was a massive surprise and blessing that came and passed all too quickly. When the hospice ambulance came to get her at 3:00 p.m., it was like a bitter flashback to when the ambulance had first taken her from home to the hospice just a few weeks ago. But the happiness and gratitude of receiving this one last Christmas gift was enough to overshadow the ongoing grief.

You see, God would not let us experience Christmas alone, or even away from our home. Oh how He loves us. It was bitter sweet to be certain, but still a huge blessing.

## One other special event

Not only were we given Christmas, but January 10 was Katie's birthday. We gathered around her hospice bed with chocolate cake, balloons and party hats one more time.

She passed four days later. 800 people packed the church worship center to share in the celebration of her transition into Heaven.

Indeed, when a Believer dies, it is a time to celebrate. Not to mourn and wear sad faces. In the next chapter I will share with you what Katie did to guarantee her eternal home in God's Country.

## Was she a strong person?

During all that she suffered through, Katie always had a positive attitude. It was not a mask. It was real. The kind of deep, positive outlook that only comes from a spiritual anchoring in the Lord.

So was she strong?

If you had asked me that question about her prior to cancer, I may have said, "No, she is not the kind of athletic person who might run a marathon or climb a mountain. In fact she hated running and never was much for exercise or working out."

But if you asked me whether she was strong after I watched her go through the cancer experience, I would have to say, "Yes. You bet. She was like a steel magnolia. She walked through the cancer and death process – and to many onlookers, made it look easy."

She was strong in the most important way we all hope to be strong as we walk through the valley of the shadow of death. There are lots of people who are strong in the body but not all are strong in the spirit.

An example of her strength and faith in God was demonstrated by this – her final log entry on her CaringBridge page – 2 Corinthians 1:3-5:

### Praise to the God of All Comfort

[3] Praise be to the God and Father of our Lord Jesus Christ, the Father of compassion and the God of all comfort, [4] who comforts us in all our troubles, so that we can comfort those in any trouble with the comfort we ourselves receive from God. [5] For just as we share abundantly in the sufferings of Christ, so also our comfort abounds through Christ.

## The grieving process can greatly vary.

God sent me another source of comfort and insight. Bob Maday was a colleague at work. He turned out to be another blessing from the Lord, a friend and mentor all in one. His wife had cancer and passed on at least a year before Katie. So he was able and willing to give me a verbal picture of what to expect each step of the cancer.

Now let me back-track for a few moments.

In the immediate aftermath of Katie's passing, I continued to have an unwavering sense of God's presence. I knew that not only was she in a great place in the hands of the Lord, now that the cancer ordeal had finally passed, so were I and the kids.

This was a theme I stressed with Matthew and Kristen – giving them a sure reassurance that God was still quite present and with us. He had not and would not forget or forsake us.

I was prepared for them to go through whatever grieving process they each needed, and was allowing myself to do the same. But what struck me was the fact that I almost didn't seem to need much of a grieving process.

You hear about people going through the stages of grief but somehow I didn't feel the need to do a lot of that. I could imagine how odd that might seem to others but I didn't want to just manufacture feelings and actions of grieving when there were none; or better yet, they had already occurred or been dealt with.

Another example of God not allowing me to be alone was the fact that He kept sending various people to be around me at key points in the journey. It was uncanny how just the right person seemed to materialize *by coincidence* at just the right time in my life. One of those people was a co-worker, Bob, introduced on the previous page.

Bob and I did not work together but we were linked by common experience: he had lost his wife from cancer about a year prior to me.

At various points along my journey, he and I would get together and just talk. It was not a formal thing but as soon as we would gather every two months or so, we just began talking like old friends.

There is a certain bonding that shared suffering brings. When you are going through something like this, you immediately have a lot in common.

Bob would give me advice and a heads-up about what may be around the corner for me, as he had been there himself. Time and time again his words of counsel were very valuable.

One such conversation with Bob was shortly after Katie's passing. I shared how I really did not seem to need to grieve as much as I would have expected.

He had exactly the insight and explanation to make sense of this for me. He explained that when someone passes from an illness like cancer – for everyone else the grieving process starts at their death, but for you, the spouse, who has been there at every step along the way, you have been grieving for a long time already. So when the person finally passes, you have already gone through most of your grieving.

It was something you did – grieving their death and loss before they actually passed away – because you could see it coming.

I couldn't have worded it as well as Bob did, but it made sense. Others were just starting their grieving but I had already gone through those stages. Also, I had my incredible dream vision experience which had a very powerful grief reduction aspect to it. As much as I might try to share my dream, there is no way I can actually give others my experience. I try my best and pray that the

Lord will do the rest, pass along insight and comfort and use my words to fulfill His purposes in the life of others.

As I described earlier, when the angel in light told me the news that she was leaving soon it brought up to the surface all the negative feelings of hurt and pain. And at the next word – all of those feelings of hurt and pain were instantly eliminated, healed and dealt with. It was quite astonishing to experience it and is still difficult to convey in words to others.

I experienced little grieving and I was intent on trying to pass along that sense of peace and calm and comfort to my kids. Since they did not have my actual dream experience and could only experience it second-hand through my words, I was never really certain how much comfort they felt and how much formal grieving they would need.

But I wanted them to know we would be ok, we were not lying down in life and becoming victims of this tragedy. We had God who loves us and is watching over us. We need not shrink back in fear or pain.

We were moving forward in life. Full speed ahead.

And that is what we did.

I am certain that others were confused by this incredible resiliency, because we all seemed to be doing amazingly well. I chalked it up to God's grace and blessing.

At this point, I want to touch on an important subject. I have not only experienced this kind of loss of a loved one – through cancer – that lasted almost five years in total. I also experienced the loss of my mother from recurring cancer and that journey lasted over a decade. I have not experienced the kind of immediate and sudden loss that many experience when a loved one passes suddenly – like from a car accident or heart attack. I do not know much about that sort of event except that I am certain it is quite different and in many ways much harder, but in other ways a bit easier.

Certainly the shock of it must be the hardest and most traumatic aspect. And then there is the likely issue of not being prepared and the wish to have been able to share some important words; for example, some last words of love.

There must be a lot of collateral injury to everyone surrounding a sudden loss. I think of the movie Collateral Beauty, a moving story starring Will Smith that explores the pain and grieving of parents at the loss of a child. I can't begin to speak much about that situation based on my own experience, except to share the ways God has worked in our lives, and is close to the broken-hearted.

I can recommend that you allow the grieving process to happen and that you try to cling to God like you have never done before. Pray for His voice, His strength, and His peace. He is a God of grace and mercy and His grace will be sufficient for you and your family. You must simply trust in Him and watch for the ways He intervenes in your struggle.

Again, John Eldredge speaks to this as he recounted in a podcast how he reacted to the sudden death of his best friend, co-author and ministry partner, Brent Curtis. They co-wrote his first book and Brent was killed in a rope-climbing accident at one of their first boot camp events years ago. John described his pain and anger that flowed immediately after the loss. He asked the usual question – why? But he remembered also to not draw away from God and shared this interesting insight. He said in your pain, you can either have God or have an explanation – but you can't have both. At least not immediately. Faced with that choice, he chose to cling to God. And that is the choice that makes all the difference. Later down the line, you may get some sort of understanding why the loss, or more likely you will have to wait until you also pass into the Kingdom of Heaven and can ask the Lord directly. But in the meantime, don't reject God. I second that advice.

God never brings on death or loss. In fact He hates it as well. He allows it just as he allows for all sorts of evil to occur on this fallen world. Allowing evil also allows for the possibility of choosing good and choosing God and that is the most important choice that we must be allowed to make in this life. Concerning death, remember how even Jesus wept at the tomb of Lazarus when He felt the pain of loss that everyone else was experiencing. And, remember, He knows the end of the story and knew that He would raise Lazarus that very day. Yet He still wept. The experience of loss, even though it is temporary, is real and He feels that emotion as well.

He shared in their loss and he shares in the feelings of loss anytime one of us loses a loved one. What is impactful in the words He shared and the visions He revealed is that our feelings of loss are just that – immediate feelings. The actual loss is not real, or is only a temporary separation.

As He said to me, you can never lose her. Let that sink in again and again – you can never lose a loved one. People, souls, just don't disappear. They go on and on, and as children of God, they go immediately to a heavenly place prepared for them. And you will see them again.

That is why He offered a remedy for death – it's called resurrection, and the offer is to all who call upon His name.

But being a *good* person will not punch anyone's ticket to Heaven. Sadly, many millions of people globally believe doing more good deeds than bad deeds is what it takes to enter Heaven.

# Chapter Twenty-One: Can Getting Into Heaven Be Guaranteed?

Absolutely.

There is no mystery how Katie qualified to enter Heaven. She had accepted Jesus as her personal Lord and Savior – long before cancer.

In my eyes – and in the eyes of others who knew her – Katie was a *good* person.

But being a *good* person will not guarantee anyone's admission into Heaven. Sadly, many millions of people globally believe doing more good deeds than bad deeds is what it takes to enter Heaven.

They find it hard to accept that the Gospel message – the Good News – requires no special deeds on our part. Rather, we need only to accept God's offer of eternal salvation.

FREE.

There is nothing we can do to earn it. Jesus made the required sacrifice for us when He died for each of us on the cross at Calvary. He arose on the third day from the grave to conquer death once and for all.

I like what Biblical Creationist Russ Miller says about God's love letter to us – the Holy Bible:

"The Bible is true, word for word, and cover to cover."

Consider what the Bible says about how to obtain eternal salvation. But first, let me stress that the saying, "All roads lead to Rome," has no application to what many people mistakenly believe: "All roads lead to God."

Jesus bluntly refuted that notion in John 14:6:

"I am the way, the truth, and the life. No one can come to the Father except through me."

The New Testament is quite clear that we cannot work our way into Heaven:
All have sinned and fall short of the glory of God. – Romans 3:23
There is no one righteous, not even one. – Romans 3:10
For the wages of sin is death. – Romans 6:23
Therefore no one will be declared righteous in [God's] sight by observing the law; rather, through the law we become conscious of sin. – Romans 3:20
As Andy Stanley states in his short book, *How good is good enough?*
"The New Testament comes right out and says what the Old Testament implies:
*No one will reach God by being good."*

## The ABC's of becoming a Christian

**A** is ADMIT you're a sinner, that you need Christ as your Savior, and that all those who call on the Lord Jesus and obey Him will be saved. You can't be saved without Him, nor add to or take from what Christ has done for you.
All have sinned and fall short of the glory of God. – Romans 3:23
But God demonstrates His own love for us in this: While we were still sinners, Christ died for us. – Romans 5:8
For the wages of sin is death. – Romans 6:23

**B** is BELIEVE the Lord Jesus Christ is the Son of the Living God. You can know He is Who He says He is by the hundreds of prophecies that came true in His Life. Many things foretold hundreds of years before His birth came true in His lifetime, and others He Himself made came true later.
For of Him and through Him and to Him *are* all things, to whom *be* glory forever. Amen. – Romans 11:36

C is CONFESS. That if you confess with your mouth the Lord Jesus and believe in your heart that God has raised Him from the dead, you will be saved. – Romans 10:9.

For with the heart one believes unto righteousness, and with the mouth confession is made unto salvation. – Romans 10:10

For whoever calls on the name of the LORD shall be saved. – Romans 10:13

Confess to the Lord and admit to yourself that you have responsibilities and that you have commitments as a Believer and follower of Jesus Christ. The more you know about the Lord Jesus Christ, the more you'll want to tell other people about Him (Romans 10:13, 11:36, John 1:1).

Remember, there is no deed or any form of work you can do to be saved. Ephesians 2: 8-9 confirms this:

[8] For it is by grace you have been saved, through faith—and this is not from yourselves, it is the gift of God— [9] not by works, so that no one can boast.

In the beginning was the Word, and the Word was with God, and the Word was God. – John 1:1 (Author's comment: This verse documents the eternalness of Jesus. He was there at the beginning. He was the Word – Logos. He was with God. He was God. The full context of the Bible passage, of which this was the first verse, includes Jesus' participation in Creation.)

I accepted Jesus Christ as my personal Lord and Savior as a young boy. Without him in my life, I could easily have become a living mess. Whatever blessings I've had – and successes in my personal and business lives – they are gifts from God. I remember saying a sinner's prayer similar to the one below. If you already are a Believer, fantastic. I look forward to seeing you in God's Country.

If you are not a Believer, and want to make sure you will be in Heaven when you die, please consider accepting God's invitation to you to have eternal life in Heaven. Truly believe Jesus Christ is the son of the living God. And confess with your mouth that you have committed your life to following Jesus.

"Lord Jesus, I know that I am a sinner, and that I do not deserve eternal life. But, I believe you died and rose from the grave to purchase a place in Heaven for me. Jesus come into my life, take control of my life, forgive my sins and save me. I am now placing my trust in you alone for my salvation and I accept your free gift of eternal life."

If you just said this prayer, and truly are sincere, please let me know via the e-mail address listed on the Internet at www.IntoGodsCountry.com. I will rejoice with the angels in Heaven.

Imagine that. What God longs for us is freedom. A free heart, free from the bondage to sin and death, free from the worry about sin and death, free from the burdens of this life that the world is constantly piling up.

# Chapter Twenty-Two: Red Pill or Blue Pill?

We all make decisions that determine where we will live forever.

If you are not yct a Believer, you learned in the previous chapter how to become one and ensure your passage to Heaven – Into God's Country.

Deciding for or against Jesus is what it boils down to. Having read this far, you know what is at stake in this decision-making process:

Eternal joy and peace.

Or eternal torment.

Heaven and Hell both exist. Believing one or both do not exist will not make them go away. This is true also in accepting one of our world's greatest lies – that God's Holy Word, the Bible, is a book of myths.

## An assessment of the world we live in.

We live in a fallen world full of darkness and deception. It's a carnival of falseness and distraction. The world encourages people to turn from God and follow their own misguided heart.

As reported in the Book of Genesis, the deception began in the Garden of Eden, initiated by Lucifer, chief of liars and the prince of darkness. Disguised as a serpent, he craftily mixed some truth with his lies to lure Eve to disobey God and eat of the forbidden fruit:

"It's ok to eat of the fruit of the Tree of Knowledge of Good and Evil. You surely won't die. Instead, you will be like God."

A bold-faced lie is easy to spot and avoid being deceived, but the most effective lies have some truth in them to make the listener believe them enough to take the bait.

The serpent was partially speaking the truth when he said, "…you will not die."

Adam and Eve did not fall over dead the moment they ate of it. They went on to live for some time, though their lives were drastically changed. Their willful disobedience poisoned their hearts and began the process of killing their hearts for God and turning their hearts from being alive to God to being cold and stony and dead to God. It did not kill their immediate physical lives, but it ended their communion and natural trust with God – and their happy, eternal life with God did die.

Those who rebel and reject God get what they have essentially asked for – a life and eternity without God.

Through Adam's participation in what is called the original sin, death entered our world.

Death was never God's plan. He wanted us to forever eat freely from the Tree of Life and fellowship with Him in the Garden of Eden. Keep this thought in mind when you get to the chapter, Heaven Comes Down.

## Adam's sin was similar to Lucifer's.

Lucifer and one-third of the angels were kicked out of Heaven in a rebellion led by Lucifer, who wanted to position himself above God. Adam, in buying into the serpent's enticement that by eating fruit from the Tree of Knowledge of Good and Evil, "You will be like God," he showed that he believed he could make better decisions than God could. What an incredible act of foolishness Adam committed. You and I grow old and die because of Adam's sin. Millions of people have been murdered because all of Adam's descendants were born with a sin nature as a result of Adam's disobedience to God.

We can thank Satan for all that is wrong and evil in our world.

But thank God that He loves us so much that He provided an antidote – eternal salvation by accepting His only begotten son, Jesus the Christ, as personal Lord and Savior.

## And just what is wrong with a little knowledge?

Isn't knowledge information a good thing?

Surely we have to believe in science. I agree with Russ Miller, founder of Creation, Evolution, and Science Ministries, who says, "True science is a Christian's best friend."

It is ironic that most of the science disciplines were founded by Christians who strongly believed in the Bible and the account in the Book of Genesis of Creation. And now most of the Science disciplines are dominated by atheists who shout out that the Bible is nothing more than a book of myths.

You know what – the Bible has strong words to say about this development. The Bible predicted the age we live in – "science falsely so-called."

1 Timothy 6:20-21 King James Version (KJV) [20] O Timothy, keep that which is committed to thy trust, avoiding profane and vain babblings, and oppositions of science falsely so called: [21] Which some professing have erred concerning the faith. Grace be with thee. Amen.

Have you noticed that reports are coming more often of creatures found alive and thriving that evolutionary-bent scientists claimed went extinct millions of years ago? And what about the recent findings of dinosaur bones with soft tissue that couldn't possibly have existed for thousands of years, let alone those many millions of years claimed?

We live in a world teeming with hocus-pocus mind games orchestrated to get us to turn against God and the Bible. But it is not knowledge of things that is the problem. Remember the full name of the tree of death?

It was called the tree of the knowledge of good and evil. In other words, it is the tree that teaches people to decide *FOR THEMSELVES* what is good or evil.

What Adam and Eve did led to a terrible result. Because when you choose that path you are placing yourself in God's position, on His throne. You are trying to be like God in that you now get to set the rules. You think you know better than God what will make life better for you. You have chosen to trust your own understanding more than God's.

A very important three-letter word tells what this line of thinking and action is:

SIN.

Calling it something else or believing that there is no such thing, just doesn't make it so. Sin is simply you choosing to ignore what God told you, and He told you these things for your own good. So, truly, if you conduct your life that way, you have decided your fate:

You have chosen to go against God. There is no middle ground. You either are choosing God or choosing against God. You can't be just a little pregnant. Either you are or you aren't.

## Look around at the world.

Do you need more illustration of how badly Adam and Eve's choice has affected our world?

Just look at how terribly people treat people when they live apart from God's love and His law. Do you see how God's laws are not a burden, but rather a blessing that keep us from turning our world into chaos and hate? If you need more reasons to accept God, spend more time on the Internet; spend more time watching your news feeds; spend more time watching the news or politics or spend time with and observe non-Believers.

I don't know of any better way to drive people to God than to spend time looking at and being among those who are far from God. I don't know about you, but the world and all its problems just send me running back to God.

When I am tempted to stray back toward the world because some small thing gets my attention, stokes my Desire, fuels any lust for anything, I try to remember to look around on any path that takes me wandering back toward the world – and when I do look around, I see the horror and pain and ugliness of what the world really offers but tries so carefully to hide. All the temptations of the world look good at first – just as the apple the Devil showed to Eve it says in scripture looked good to eat.

Appearances can be deceiving.

Just because something looks good or a life style appears to be good, doesn't mean it is. It is a trap, a deception from the Evil One designed to fool you, to get you to turn from God and follow the desires of your own heart. And what you may not remember at that moment is that our own hearts have this wicked streak in them that when we are apart from God, we are apt to make a foolish choice.

## Are you on God's team?

You are either on God's team or you aren't. No one is allowed to sit on the sidelines of this ultimate game. You get to choose your team and play your part but in the end only one team wins.

Choose wisely and live well.

If you choose to live in the world and be like the world and shun the ways of God – He in His grace will give you what you want:

Your life without God – for eternity.

But if you choose God you are claiming His free offer to restore yourself, to get a new heart, to rejoin the team you were born to be a part of. And you will receive the new heart and new life and become part of the resurrection story that God promised to all who simply believe in Jesus in their hearts

And confess His name. If you confess Christ's name He promises that when you face your judgment day He will confess your name. Imagine that – you will be hauled into the judge's chambers and God will not allow anyone who chooses evil to just waltz right into Heaven a free and happy man or lady. No – there will be judgment and all your earthly deeds – those that people know about and those that only God knows about – they will all be laid bare for you and God and anyone else in court to see and evaluate.

If you don't have Jesus by your side it will be like trying to defend yourself in court with no attorney and no witnesses in your favor. The case will be open and shut and you will lose – and lose forever. But if Jesus is on your side He said He would confess your name before God.

Do you get that?

He will declare you forgiven and righteousness enough to be pardoned and to gain entry into Heaven. His blood on the cross was an atoning sacrifice for *YOUR* sins. For your bad decisions throughout your life.  This is the only way and it can be your story.

## Think of the movie The Matrix.

Two pills are set before Mr. Anderson.  The red pill and the blue pill.  He is given a choice.  You can either choose the blue pill and go back to sleep and back into the world – the world by the way that is shown to actually be asleep, and in bondage.

Or you can choose the red pill and you will see the truth about how far the rabbit trail really goes.

Do you remember the movie?  The red pill woke Mr. Anderson up and showed him what was really going on.

Those who were asleep, and chose to be asleep by taking the blue pill were the deceived ones, getting the life sucked out of them by an evil power.

If you choose the world that is what happens. You live for a time, you get the life sucked out of you and you are discarded and die when you are no longer useful to the Beastly Machine of Evil.

But Mr. Anderson chose wisely and bravely a path that he had to take on faith – that he couldn't know for certain where it would lead.  He chose the red pill representing a heart that is alive and not a cold and stony blue heart that represents deadness in the world.

And that choice made all the difference.  Mr. Anderson got a new name, Neo, which means new.  He became a new creation. And he grew in his new life and learned of the powers he had as a result of that new life – powers that included being able to control bullets fired at him, and  how to overcome the evil one and the evil system.

If you've seen The Matrix, did you catch the comparisons to Jesus Christ that are made with the lead character Neo?

It is a powerful story because it derives its power from the most powerful story ever written – God's story. The Matrix movie is a type of the Gospel, and Neo is a Christ figure. He overcame the Matrix to set us all free.

Choosing the red pill is like saying, "Yes," to Jesus Christ. Choosing the blue pill is like saying, "No."

Scripture has a passage that says He pleads for each of us to make the right choice. "Behold, I set before you blessings and curses, life and death – choose life that you may live."

All of your life boils down to that one choice, just as Adam and Eve's life boiled down to that one choice. Choose life. Choose to eat of the Tree of Life and NOT of the Tree of Knowledge.

That is the bottom line my friends. It is not any more complicated than that. You have one choice to make. Choose well and choose life.

## These are not valid excuses to shun God.

"I'm too old."

"God won't want me because of the bad things I've done."

I know of a man who was an atheist for many decades before accepting Jesus Christ as his personal Lord and Savior past the age of 80. For over 20 years he used both of the above excuses. Two books that had heavy impacts on his decision-making process were Lee Strobel's *The Case for Christ*; also, *371 Days That Scarred Our Planet* by Russ Miller with Jim Dobkins.

He bought batches of both books and gave them to his old war buddies who were still alive.

King David in the Bible is a classic example of a man who was a murderer and adulterer who sincerely repented of his sins.

My favorite Bible scripture is part of what David wrote in Psalm 119 where he says, "I run in the path of your commands." Meaning that he is eager to follow the Lord; to do what He says to do, to avoid doing what He says to avoid, and to go where He is leading. And how to do so eagerly – not meandering, not delaying, not getting sidetracked, not even walking – but running, moving with eagerness.

That is how my experience and realization of God's love has transformed me.

And David continues on to answer why he is so fired up and passionately following after God: "...because you have set my heart free."

Imagine that. What God longs for us is freedom. A free heart, free from the bondage to sin and death, free from the worry about sin and death, free from the burdens of this life that the world is constantly piling up.

Scripture warns that before coming to Christ we all have a heart that is wicked and seeks only after sin. But after we come to Christ it really is like having open heart surgery. We are new creatures with new hearts.

Here is a portion of Psalm 119:

[32]I run in the path of Your commands,
for You have broadened my understanding.
[33]Teach me, Lord, the way of Your decrees,
that I may follow it to the end.
[34]Give me understanding, so that I may keep Your law
and obey it with all my heart.
[35]Direct me in the path of Your commands,
for there I find delight.
[36]Turn my heart toward Your statutes
and not toward selfish gain.
[37]Turn my eyes away from worthless things;
preserve my life according to Your word.
[38]Fulfill Your promise to Your servant,
so that You may be feared.
[39]Take away the disgrace I dread,
for Your laws are good.
[40]How I long for Your precepts!
In your righteousness preserve my life.
[41]May Your unfailing love come to me, Lord,
Your salvation, according to Your promise;

[42]then I can answer anyone who taunts me,
for I trust in Your word.
[43]Never take Your word of truth from my mouth,
for I have put my hope in Your laws.
[44]I will always obey Your law,
for ever and ever.
[45]I will walk about in freedom,
for I have sought out Your precepts.

Consider this promise made by the prophet Isaiah centuries before Jesus invaded our world as a human:

"For behold, I create new heavens and a new earth; and the former shall not be remembered or come to mind." – Isaiah 65:17

# Chapter Twenty-Three: Heaven Comes Down

Upon physical death and entry into Heaven – God's Country – total restoration is completed for all Believers:

No more tears.
No more sorrow.
No more death.
No more fears.
No more disease.
No more pain.
No more heartache.
No more age wrinkles.
No more negatives.
All things will be made new, including a perfect you.

Consider the promise God made via the prophet Isaiah centuries before Jesus invaded our world as a human:
"For behold, I create new heavens and a new earth; and the former shall not be remembered or come to mind." – Isaiah 65:17

## Something really super happens before this restoration.

At the moment a person accepts Jesus Christ as his or her personal Lord and Savior, this new Believer instantly is a citizen of Heaven.

This person no longer is a citizen of this world which still is under the rule of the Prince of Darkness, Lucifer, who was thrown out of Heaven along with one-third of the angels who joined in the rebellion against God.

Unfortunately, a lot of professing Christians continue to act like citizens of this world, which is coming apart at the seams due to the increasing depravity of mankind.

Here's what the Bible says we need to do to secure this new citizenship:

John 3:3 [3] Jesus replied, "Very truly I tell you, no one can see the kingdom of God unless they are born again."

Matthew 3:2 [2] and saying, "Repent, for the kingdom of heaven has come near."

Matthew 7:21 [21] Not everyone who says to me, 'Lord, Lord,' will enter the kingdom of heaven, but only the one who does the will of my Father who is in heaven.

Philippians 3:20 [20] But our citizenship is in heaven. And we eagerly await a Savior from there, the Lord Jesus Christ...

Those who study and teach the unending truths proclaimed in the Bible are more and more getting excited about what God promises He will do about Heaven.

## Heaven Comes Down

Read the account of Heaven coming down to the new earth near the end of the Book of Revelation.

The New Jerusalem is one name it's often called; also, the City Foursquare. Its dimensions are awesome, usually considered to be about 1,500 miles by 1,500 miles by 1,500 miles.

When you read John's description of Heaven, keep some basics in mind.

For example, why are there twelve gates – three on each side – if it is not meant for residents of Heaven to freely go in and out?

And if the river of life flows out from Heaven onto the new earth, isn't it reasonable to think that God created the new earth for the enjoyment of Heaven's residents?

With our every-day human bodies and frailties, I do not believe we can even begin to imagine the creativeness and beauty of the new earth. I like to imagine it as the Garden of Eden squared.

I get goose bumps just thinking about it.

There is a book – ALL THINGS NEW by bestselling author/public speaker John Eldredge – that talks about the new heavens and new earth. If reading that book does not get you excited about Heaven, I suspect you might need a new excitement gauge installed in you.

Or read one of his earlier works titled EPIC. It is a little book that tells the gospel story like a play in four acts. The fourth section, where he describes the Kingdom of Heaven, is perhaps one of the most powerful and exciting descriptions based on biblical insights that I have ever heard. In fact, there is a DVD version where John, the author, reads his book on stage as in a one-man play. Shortly after Katie passed, I sat my kids down and we watched that portion of the DVD.

I could think of no better description to read or hear portrayed than the words Eldredge used to describe the Kingdom of Heaven – God's Country.

We have much to look forward to and I wanted my children to know their mom was in a fantastic place – a place where the grass was greener. And that they too should eagerly await and look forward to the day when they will transition into that place.

If it took standing in a line that wrapped around our planet to get into Heaven, I'd rush right now as fast as I could to get in that line. But, fortunately, that is not necessary. If you've already made the decision to accept Jesus Christ as your personal Lord and Savior, we will celebrate the wedding supper of the Lamb together in Heaven.

It will be the most joyous party ever.

He connects the dots and shows us things in advance, so that when the time comes, we know it is God, and know what we are called to do.

# Chapter Twenty-Four: What I learned About How God Works

This Hallmark of God is well worth repeating:

God never gives us more than we can handle. Or said more correctly, God never gives us more than we can handle with Him by our side.

He does give us more than we can handle alone, on our own under our own power. That is exactly what He does do when we try to be a lone wolf. He sends just enough affliction that pushes us beyond what we can handle without Him, so that we can turn to Him in our hour of need.

## Eleventh-hour God

You might have heard the phrase, "We have an eleventh-hour God."

To me it feels like God sometimes uses brinksmanship. He brings us to the brink of disaster to get us to let go of our false hopes and gods and cling to the only true hope – Himself.

God tells us in His Word, the Bible:

"You will find Me when you seek Me with all your heart."

## God shows up in the nick of time.

He formed my men's group 30 days before the cancer siege began.

He sent Jamie the morning I planned to visit mortuaries and cemeteries alone.

And through Chick-fil-A, He provided Ann to help at the exact time I began to feel overwhelmed by circumstances.

He had planned these means of help all along. "I will never leave you or forsake you."

## God's timing

The net effect of God's timing is that it often seems like *bullet time*. Bullet time is a movie term that refers to a special effect that was first made popular in the movie *The Matrix*.

It is when an action scene is slowed down so much that you can see all the intricate movements happen in ultra-slow motion of an instant in real life. For instance, in that movie, you can see the actual bullets fly out of the gun barrel and whirl past the head of the main character, Neo, and even see the rotation of the bullets and the sound waves around them as they travel. It is a way of seeing a lot of detail in slow motion that really happens superfast in real time.

God's timing can be like that – you feel like things are whizzing past you but God is actually controlling all sorts of things on a micro level, but you can't see all of that happening.

Or sometimes it may seem the opposite. You are seeing things go painstakingly slow, but God is moving in the larger picture and it all seems to go slow until one moment when everything collides together and things happen. Sometimes it is a roller-coaster ride dipping into deep valleys that seem painfully slow then burst rocket-fast onto mountain tops.

God works through hardship. He does His work, draws others into fellowship with Him, and starts ministries through hardship. Hardship leads to building strong character, which leads to Godliness and holiness.

## My grace is sufficient.

As you know by reading this far, through God's hand on my life through my dream, and through the dreams and visions of the other adults and the 10-year-old girl, I daily identify with Paul after he had his Road to Damascus experience with Jesus Christ, who told Paul, "My grace is sufficient."

I try to make "My grace is sufficient" my daily, sustaining theme. This provides continuing comfort and peace to me. If I ever realize I'm about to have a pity-party, all I need to do to snap out of it is to think of the incredible hardships and persecutions Paul endured.

Jesus Christ truly was Paul's all in all.

## God can turn Evil deeds into good results.

A choice example is Joseph in the Book of Genesis. His brothers sold him into slavery in Egypt. Years later when they next saw their brother, Joseph was administrator over all of Egypt, second in power only to Pharaoh.

God's ultimate use of Evil to achieve a spectacular end result is reported in the Book of Revelation. He uses the Evil Trinity – Satan, The Anti-Christ, and the False Prophet – and an incredible array of supernatural events orchestrated by God to literally trash our planet, and drastically reduce earth's human population.

This happens during the seven-year period called the Tribulation. The second of the two 3-1/2-year periods usually is termed The Great Tribulation. That is the worst – and most terrifying time – to ever live in throughout history.

I urge you to read for yourself the Book of Revelation to find out what will happen to our planet. It is all planned out by God and foretold. He keeps His promises. Prophecy after prophecy has come true. I see no reason for God to tell us anything that will not come true.

I'm one of those people who believe "God said it. I believe it. That settles it."

## God plans things in advance.

Sometimes incredibly far in advance, as witness His plans for new heavens and a new earth.

He hung the stars and planets in space, all in perfect harmony. He made it all – Ex Nihilo – from nothing by spoken word.

So is it really any wonder that He lines up experiences throughout our lives that connect with His purposes and prepares us for what is to come, or for His new role for us to fulfill?

He connects the dots and shows us things in advance, so that when the time comes, we know it is God, and know what we are called to do. I have heard life with God described as a divine partnership. He guides us and we do our part to follow His lead. We get to choose whether we are in step with Him or out of step. He is a patient dance partner, always working to teach us the right moves, but we do get to choose whether to advance or stay where we are. Eventually the hardships of life probably work together with God's prompting to lead us to that place of surrender where we finally let go and let God take the lead.

As He tells us in the Bible, Isaiah 55: 8-9 –

"For my thoughts are not your thoughts, neither are your ways my ways, declares the Lord.

"As the heavens are higher than the earth, so are my ways higher than your ways and my thoughts than your thoughts."

## He provided Bible verses for virtually every situation.

The 23$^{rd}$ Psalm is the Bible passage that describes perfectly how I felt – and still feel – about the cancer journey with Katie.

*A Psalm of David.*

[1]The LORD *is* my shepherd;
I shall not want.
[2] He makes me to lie down in green pastures;
He leads me beside the still waters.
[3] He restores my soul;
He leads me in the paths of righteousness
for His name's sake.

[4] Yea, though I walk through the valley of the shadow of death,
I will fear no evil;
for You *are* with me;
Your rod and Your staff, they comfort me.

[5] You prepare a table before me in the presence of my
enemies;
You anoint my head with oil;
my cup runs over.
[6] Surely goodness and mercy shall follow me
all the days of my life;
and I will dwell in the house of the LORD
forever.

## God works in the details.

Over and over I've learned that God works in the details. He is
certainly not the absentee God, clockmaker I used to think He was.

He cares about every detail of my life.

He wants me to want Heaven.

And He has assured me in many ways that Heaven is real, that
Katie is there, and there is no reason for me to fear death.

I have a fantastic eternity awaiting me.

Will you be there?

There was another specific aspect of my final prayer to the Lord that night. I said, "Fine – I will go and speak to these people – but I have no idea how I will get an audience with them. I hardly know any of them, much less have a strong personal connection where I can just start talking about such weighty matters as their faith and Heaven in the context of their struggle with cancer. Just who am I to say or do such things? So, Lord, I need you to open those doors, and make these connections. I can't do it alone."

# Chapter Twenty-Five: The story was not over yet

I thought the story was over. But – again – God, in His never-ending, uniquely-creative way, had other plans.

My dream experience was the most powerful spiritual event I had ever experienced. Now, in the wake of Katie's passing, little did I know that the second-most powerful spiritual experience was just around the corner.

God had more to reveal and to accomplish through me.

Remember where the story left off, way back in Chapter Three when a new church member invited me and all the members of my Sunday School class to a Super Bowl party in his home?

Do you remember what was revealed and what was asked in the dream that the party host shared with me?

## Let me reset the stage.

As soon as I walked in the door, the homeowner and host of the party, Brent Merritt and his wife Mary, pulled me aside and told me about a dream he'd had that same morning in which Katie told him she was in Heaven and everything was wonderful.

She also asked him to tell me to talk to his neighbor's wife. That was several weeks after Katie's passing. After Brent and Mary told me their story, I discovered that they had not heard of my own dream or of any of the dreams of the others. So, rather than rejoin the party already in progress throughout their home, we and a few others gathered in a quiet portion of their house, their formal living room.

As Brent describes it, the TV was turned off in the fourth quarter of a one-point game while I then shared with him, and the others who had gathered around, my dream and the dreams and visions that the others had shared with me.

Well, the story of what happened that day did not end there. It got interesting in ways I had not expected.

## First, a quick review of what had been happening.

With Katie in God's Country, I went through a lot of readjusting:

From a routine of going to work, picking up the kids, heading to hospice, and interacting with relatives who were in town to trying to find a new *normal*. Just a lot of things to do, to just help the kids get resettled into a new reality, as well as myself.

I had returned to work, but eased slowly back into the flow of things. I had many conversations with friends and colleagues, who were just walking alongside me, helping me in the immediate aftermath of the funeral, and everything.

What started to emerge in the following weeks was that I was keenly aware of other people who were going through hardship. I noticed that I almost preferred to spend time with people who were dealing with or had dealt with some sort of adversity. I thought of it as *the company of the afflicted*. It may sound weird, but I related to them much more closely than to people who were just living a carefree life and hadn't been through any significant trial.

Perhaps it is a camaraderie like those who have been through a battle, much the way military veterans have a special bond. I just felt I could relate to them better and deeper than other people and was even drawn to be around others in their time of crisis. Also, the daily talking that made up most conversations just seemed too banal and pointless, given all the powerful spiritual events I had just gone through. It felt like most people seemed busy with insignificant distractions, while those going through hardship or who had been through hardship, had a certain maturity and wisdom that I just preferred to be around. Through an avalanche of experience gained, I also felt I was so full of resources that it was starting to feel like a new ministry for me.

The wives in two other specific families came to my attention. Both were in late-stage cancer situations similar to my story – each wife had recurring cancer and the husband was doing his best to care-give. To me, it was more than mere coincidence that these families who were somewhat connected with me were going through this at this time – it felt like a God-incidence.

One lady was Kassie, who was a receptionist at a major corporation. She was a person of quiet dignity who was always in a pleasant disposition who greeted visitors and answered the main phone down in the main lobby of that company's corporate building. I had met her at that company.

Two years prior, I ran into her at a very unusual place and learned something that she had asked me to keep in confidence. This was during the remission period for my wife and one of the things that she had been very involved with was participating on our church's Relay for Life team.

Relay for Life was an annual fundraising event held by the local chapter of the American Cancer Society. Churches, local businesses, and civic organizations sponsored teams that set up booths, sold fundraising items and participated in a 24-hour event. That overnight event was part rally, part vigil and part group therapy for those affected by the disease.

The typical set-up involved a large oval track about the size of a high school running track with a main stage and an emcee, local musicians, food vendors, and tents from each sponsoring organization lining both sides of the track. One way supporters contributed was to purchase luminaria (paper bags with candles in them). These would be placed around the track and burn all night, each bag representing a current patient or former cancer patient.

It was a pretty uplifting event that people from all around the community would come out to support. Anyone could go, but most people who attended were often family and friends of people who were associated with the cancer experience. It was a frighteningly large event – which speaks to the massive segment of the population that is impacted by cancer of some sort.

Anyhow, it was while walking around this track that I ran into Kassie among the crowd of people. I naturally asked her why she was there, thinking she might say she perhaps had a relative fighting cancer or that she was part of her church's support team. Kassie was a young woman in her 30's who always looked like the picture of health. I was shocked when she whispered in my ear that, actually, she had had a "touch of cancer."

I thought – a touch of cancer – that is an odd way to put it. It was as if she had caught a touch of the flu – you know, a light case that was almost not worth mentioning. But, hello, this was cancer! I really had never heard anyone describe their experience with cancer as a light touch. Then again, I knew she was a person of very deep faith – she was one of those strong silent types that just exuded faith in the Lord. I pictured her attending a very intense sort of church – that probably spent a lot of time in the Word, and spent many evenings at the church.

Ever since that event, I had kept in closer contact with her, but we never discussed her little revelation of cancer and I never shared it with anyone else.

## Fast forward after Katie's passing and my return to work.

Soon after I returned to work, I heard from a mutual friend, Alice, who knew Kassie and shared with me that Kassie was out on long-term sick leave. I asked why and learned that she had stage 4 cancer in her bones. Alice began to fill me in on what had transpired in Kassie's life over the past many months.

Since the news of Kassie's cancer was apparently out in the open, I admitted that I had been aware of the initial diagnosis for some time because Kassie had what she described as *a touch of cancer*, but I really didn't know any other details. Alice brought me up to speed. Basically, Kassie's first discovery of cancer was in her breast, and she and her husband had turned to both a medical and a homeopathic – and especially to a faith-healing approach.

Over time the cancer seemed to disappear.

It was not clear how much formal medical treatment she had vs. how much dietary approach; but one thing was clear, they had trusted in the healing that they prayed for from the Lord.

This must have happened before or during the time I ran into Kassie at the Relay for Life event. She showed little sign of having cancer and frankly kept it to herself very well. Only her closest friends knew anything of it and, of course, their close-knit church prayer group.

But now, two years later, the cancer had returned and spread to other places, mainly in her bones. Apparently she had had more than just a touch of cancer. I learned that she had suffered a spontaneous fracture of her femur that kept her out of work for some time while that was addressed with surgery and more cancer medicines. Her situation had turned worse and she was on medical leave as the cancer was affecting more and more of her body.

Alice was also a friend of mine and had heard of some of my dream and vision stories. She also was a person of deep and abiding faith and was fascinated and drawn in by my stories.

## So with all that background, I can get back to the story.

I was back at work and Alice made a point to reach out to me to encourage me to perhaps share my story with Kassie and her husband. On one hand, I was eager to share it. On the other hand, I was often hesitant to share it for one reason:

I recognized quite well that in many ways, the outcome of my story – the fact that my wife passed from cancer – might not be the answer to prayer that most people or anyone is really wanting to hear if they or a loved one is in a similar circumstance. They want physical healing and recovery now, in this life, or at least a long trajectory of life that pushed out the unwanted news of death as long as possible. I am keenly aware that many people are not ready or don't have ears to hear anything beyond what they are earnestly praying for.

I always pray for others' healing and pray in agreement with their desires for specific physical healing, but I am also open to the idea that God may not always grant that kind of healing. Sometimes He has other plans. And here is something that may be hard for people to grasp – but I wish I could get people to grapple with this concept:

**What if God is indeed planning to heal your loved one, but that healing will be accomplished in the Kingdom of Heaven? In a real sense, isn't that the most complete and permanent sort of healing?**

I know those are radical words, but it is how I think and feel after my experience. God can and does heal in the body, but when a Believer dies and passes into Heaven, they are healed indeed and in full. That is not the answer most people want or are ready to hear, unless the loved one is old and or is in great suffering. But as Christians we must be open to that. Hold on to this idea, because I am going to come back to it again later.

## Pause the story about Kassie.

Also going on in these first few weeks after Katie's passing was a story of another family. This wife was named Shirley. Her daughter was a grade school classmate of my daughter Kristen, which meant the teacher had two students with mothers dealing with late-stage cancer – one with breast cancer, and another with pancreatic cancer.

When the teacher of these two girls prayed about the situation, about why she had two students dealing with this difficult situation, instead of saying, "Why me?" she described to me that in her prayer time she felt it was a distinct honor and sacred responsibility that she felt she had been called to walk in, to help these two girls in any way she could.

She was a diligent, caring teacher, and went the extra mile for these two girls. She helped arrange for them to spend time with the school counselor and kept me and the other parents well informed of anything she felt was important. This helped us to all partner together to help shepherd the hearts of these two young girls who were going through something so traumatic.

The teacher was yet another God-send to our family – I mean that literally. She was sent by God and we were certain both girls were in the same class for a reason, not by coincidence.

## It's interesting how God works.

He can choose to work through anyone in any circumstance. What happened was that these two girls, my daughter Kristen and the other girl, became friends – and ended up being a great support for one another. Over the years since, they have remained friends.

Pancreatic cancer can run its course and be fatal pretty quickly, but in this case, Shirley had successfully battled it for over a year, going in and out of the hospital, but seeming to bounce back.

What made the other girl's story all the more heart-wrenching was that she had been an adopted child. Her birth-mother had passed away long before. So, in a real sense, she was losing her mother all over again – a second time. It was heartbreaking to think about. But she seemed to have a resiliency and found comfort and friendship with my daughter.

I remember praying and marveling how the Lord had gently protected us during our ordeal and how He was already able to use Kristen as a way to minister to this girl. And the ministry seemed to work in both directions – she also was a source of comfort to Kristen. Theirs was a ministry of fellowship – pure and simple. Only they and God know the deep conversations that must have transpired between them.

At the same time I was returning to work and learning about Kassie's story, I was also hearing from sources in the school that Shirley was going into a serious phase of her cancer – with potentially not long to live.

So all this to say that I was definitely feeling drawn into the lives of other people – or as I used to put it, our orbits were being drawn together. I had a sense that God was prompting me to connect with these people and share something – my story, words of comfort.

**But – How? When?**

I was living with this growing awareness when I made the last-minute decision to attend that Super Bowl party. Which, if you remember, I never actually intended to go to. It was only by what felt like a last-minute change of my mind, after the game had already started, that I *chose* to go to the party. I wondered why I felt a prompting to change my mind and go. And when I did –

BOOM!

I get told this fantastic dream within minutes of stepping into the house.

After spending the evening recounting the highlights of all these dreams, I was exhausted, but also keyed up. In some ways I was also starting to panic a bit. I felt like a wire that had too much electricity flowing through it. All this spiritual talk and all this connectivity to those going through a similar cancer journey was building up in me like an electric charge. I sensed God at work in all of this but I had no idea how to handle it all or what the Lord was really wanting me to do.

When I went home after that party, my head was spinning. I tried to recount in my mind what I had just heard from the Meritts. If I had recalled correctly, I was supposed to connect with a friend or neighbor of the Merrits – someone I had never met and had utterly no other connection to – except that they were dealing with cancer. All I could think to do was to call my friend Jim Weathers, whom I sometimes referred to as Moses, because he walked so closely with God. Yes, I figured a conversation with Moses was in order.

## Three families

It had become very obvious:

God had brought three families into my orbit, or me into their orbit. Clearly, He was doing this for a reason. But I had no idea specifically what He wanted me to do or share or how to do it. I was overwhelmed. I was starting to wonder if the Lord had some new assignment for me to be one who counsels people with cancer.

It was not a role I felt qualified to do, but who was I to question what God may be up to?

I called Jim quite late on that Sunday night after returning home from the Super Bowl party, and to my great relief, he answered.

He listened patiently as I recounted all of this to him.

About the wife of the neighbor of the Merrits; as well as the two other ladies with late-stage cancer – Kassie and Shirley.

After I stopped talking, Jim simply said that he believed as I did that God was up to something here, that I should pray and stay close to God and that he, Jim, would walk alongside me through whatever was ahead.

Again, God would not let me walk through something like this alone – he sent Moses, or rather Jim, to be a friend and mentor and guide. As a former pastor, Jim was well experienced at talking to people and offering counsel. Also, as one who walked closely with God, he also had access to some deep insights. Come to think of it, I was starting to realize that I too was walking closely with God and had some direct connections and insights as well.

Here is a secret:

It is God who is near at hand to each of us and we all have access to His wisdom and insight. We only have to remember to ask Him. It says in scripture, ask and you will receive, knock and the door will be open.

Elsewhere it says, you do not receive because you do not ask. So, the implication is – Just ask. Often that means ask and wait – wait upon the Lord. Wait for an answer or a prompting. Yes, it helps to stay steeped in scripture – remember, it is part of God's language and His vocabulary. Often, He will answer you ... by directing or leading you to a scripture verse. The Bible is, in some way, a decoding device about God. Whatever you need to know is contained somewhere in scripture – you usually only need a prompting or a pointer to which verse to read.

As I hung up the phone with Jim, sometime around midnight, I began to feel better. Although I had no idea what was going to happen next, at least I felt a wave of peace wash over me and knew that somehow the Lord would lead me wherever He wanted me to go. I surrendered my will and left it all to Him.

I appreciated deeply the company that Jim was offering.

So, before I began to close my eyes to drift off to sleep, I prayed a very specific prayer. I said to the Lord, "OK, I see that You are prompting me to say something to each of these families – but, Lord, I have no idea how I am going to have an opportunity or gain an audience with each of them – I barely know them or don't know them at all, likewise with their husbands. So You will have to help me make contact with them. And, though I am not sure what precisely I am to say, I do trust You and know that You will give me the words to say when I need them."

This is more of that divine partnership sort of prayer I described earlier – where we surrender our will and our time, but we also expect and ask God to do His part as well. We do not demand or dictate, but we simply ask and trust that the Lord will act and open the doors that need to be opened. Again, in all things we are to not be anxious about anything but in all things, with prayer and petition and thanksgiving make our requests of God. And the peace of God which passes understanding will guard our hearts and mind in Christ Jesus. That is what I was trying to do.

I also was trusting and relying on God to give me the necessary words at the moment they were needed. I had learned the truth of another passage of scripture, 1 Peter 3:16 that says, in part, "Always be prepared to give an answer to everyone who asks you to give the reason for the hope that you have."

We should have thought through and be prepared with the sorts of things we will say when others ask us about our faith – not just what church we belong to or when we had a conversion experience, but some of the reasons behind that.

This usually means being willing to see and describe actual experiences, times in our own lives, when God showed up and when scriptural passages proved to be true and real in our own lives.

God gives us these experiences to bless us and to serve as illustrations for others when they ask or need to hear our own stories of faith.

People want to know why you believe, what prompted you to make that statement of faith, and how the Lord has become real to you in your life. As one great preacher, Dr. Frank Harrington, once said in a sermon:

"On one hand it is easy to ask church members about their faith – they will often tell you where they attend church and for how long.

"But if you really want a conversation stopper, follow up that question with this question – 'Yes, but when did you really start doing business with Jesus Christ?'"

His point was that too often church goers may not really be doing much business with Jesus Christ. They may have a surface relationship or practice only and not truly be turning to and consulting and praying to and listening to and walking with the Lord. A true Believer who learns to abide in the Lord, does these things and walks closely with Him. Like a sheep that doesn't stray far from the shepherd. It is people like this that are probably more prepared for the questions that the scripture says to prepare for. Again, it said to always be prepared to give a reason for the hope that you have. And elsewhere it says we should not worry about what to say because the Spirit will give us the words we need. This can sound like a contradiction – on one hand telling us to be prepared and on the other hand saying the Spirit will speak to and through us.

**So which is it?  I think it is both.**

In essence, this is the point of this book. I want to give my story and give to you lots of the reasons that I live with such hope and why all my hope is founded upon Jesus Christ. All of my experiences confirm what the Bible has said to be true. This is why I am sharing this with you – that you too might understand what I do and that you would build upon the truths I share and discover and verify them for yourself in your own life.

## Divine Partnership

Another thing I have learned about how the Lord operates – it is something I call a divine partnership, or perhaps I have heard someone else call it that. The idea is that God could do all things Himself, but He prefers to partner with His children to accomplish His work in this world. Take the great commission as a huge example. God certainly could light up the sky with a blazing sign in multiple languages to spread the gospel message – just blanket the world in a massive infomercial.

But He doesn't choose to do that. Instead, He deputized His followers and gave them the most far-reaching mission statement on earth: to go to all the earth and preach the Gospel. In other words, He wants to partner with us to be His agents on earth. What an awesome honor and responsibility.

Likewise, even on smaller things in our own lives, He could do it all for us, but He wants to train us up, to mature us, and give us the opportunity to be like Him – so instead, He often partners with us. He partners with us on our own training and development, letting us more or less dictate the speed at which we learn about Him and grow into His likeness. He also partners with us when it comes to reaching out to others, serving the needy, missioning around the world, or just speaking a necessary and encouraging word to another person who needs it.

I have given many illustrations of how God prompted others to swing into action to come to my aid. I was a huge recipient of literally hundreds of people's acts of kindness toward me and my family. Those people were all or almost all prompted by the Lord. Some were very obvious, like the day Jamie called me out of the blue saying he had been prompted that we would be doing something together on the day I had told no one, but had planned to quietly slip away and look into funeral arrangements. Others were so much more mundane – like providing childcare, or bringing me breakfast when I was hungry.

I saw it and learned to recognize it over and over, and wow has it changed my viewpoint on how God and other people work – I am super grateful for everything that was done for me and now I am much more inclined myself to offer help to others when I sense a need or especially when I feel a prompting to do so.

Again, it is a divine partnership:

God does His part and we do ours.

That is how it is supposed to work. We become mentally prepared and yielded to what God is prompting us to do and He makes up for any shortcomings we may have. It is a both, and not an either/or kind of thing.

So often people are hard of hearing to God, and so wrapped up in the cares and concerns of their own lives and desires, that they neither hear nor respond to the call to partner with God.

It is a shame on multiple levels:

- It becomes a life that is inward focused.
- It leads to a life that is selfish and unfulfilling.
- And it also results in a life that never truly lives as God intended.

You miss all sorts of opportunities and blessings that only come when you partner with the Lord and bless others. It is more blessed to give than to receive. Really, it is almost a statement of an automatic principle – like gravity – that you will be blessed the more you give.

So, this final prayer was one of submission, agreement and divine partnership. I was, in effect, saying, "OK, I will go where You want me to go and say or do what You want me to say or do – but You, O Lord, must lead me. You must open the right doors. You must be a light unto my feet and show me the way."

And you know what?

He did.

And He will for you, if you only ask.

When those words were spoken something in my soul just jumped back in shock. What are the chances that this is the same person, and that she is now at the same hospice that we had been at for six weeks leading up to Katie's passing?

# Chapter Twenty-Six: Hey, Eric, what's going on lately?

The next day was Monday. I went to work and started to relate this situation to a few close friends. I told them how I had no idea how on earth I would get to talk with three different families, each struggling with cancer, and what I would say. I told myself and others over and over that day, "The only story I have to tell is my story."

On Tuesday I got a surprise phone call. I looked down and saw the name of the mother of my daughter's friend at school – Shirley, the other mom with cancer. I had never gotten a call from her.

I was a bit startled, but managed a tentative, "Hello."

The voice on the other end of the phone said, "Hello, this is Shirley ..."

I thought for a moment that I had recently heard she was back in the hospital for more treatment for her pancreatic cancer. I figured she had returned home.

She continued, "The girls want to have a sleepover this weekend. I'm checking to see if that is OK."

I replied, "Yes, that sounds good, but I usually have met the parents of any friend she is going to have a sleepover at. Could we meet up sometime?"

"Sure – how about this evening?"

I agreed to stop over after work to get to know them. The entire call lasted about a minute. As soon as we hung up, I realized that, unwittingly, I had just made an arrangement to meet this stranger in person – cancer patient number one. That seemed odd, but fortunate. Perhaps I would get my chance to talk with her then.

Now a pause. I will get back later to my meeting with Shirley.

The following day was Wednesday. Nothing happened.

Then came Thursday and another surprise. Alice, the Chick-fil-A colleague who knew Kassie, the other cancer victim, came to me and said, "Hey, I was thinking of bringing some dinner by

Kassie's house this evening. I was wondering of you would like to come with me? Perhaps you could share some of your story with them."

I must have given her a blank look for a moment, because she had to prompt me again for an answer. I said, "Sure."

She said, "Great, I will meet you there around 6:30. I will bring dinner for all of us and you bring yourself and your stories."

I thought, "This is interesting. This is cancer patient number two and I am apparently going over for dinner at her house. How about that. Perhaps I will have a chance to talk with her and her husband then – in fact, I've been asked to do so. This was pretty easy."

Another pause. I will get back to Kassie later.

The following day was Friday, my favorite day of the week because Friday mornings are the mornings I get to go to the Log House and meet with my band of brothers – my close friends who make up my Bible study group. These are the men who are like your platoon mates in a fire fight. I know they have my back and that I will have theirs. They are true spiritual brothers and warriors as well.

Typically, the morning unfolds in three segments. We begin by reading the daily devotional for that date from Oswald Chamber's book, *My Utmost for His Highest*. Then we have an open time where people can speak up to the whole group about any prayer requests, or praise reports they may have on their mind or heart. Sometimes people share current events as well – like any upcoming guest speakers coming to the area, or some other bit of information that the whole group might be interested in – but this is not a group social time. It is primarily for prayer requests. Then after that, we break up into small groups of three or four men, and pray together based on what requests we just heard or anything else that comes to mind or heart. The last segment is straight Bible study.

On this particular day, something out of the ordinary happened and it was so striking that I can remember it in perfect detail, almost as clearly as I can recount my dream experience.

### It happened like this.

After most of the guys seemed to have spoken any prayer concerns, but just before we were to break into small groups to begin praying, a guy from across the room, Russ Breault, called out loud and clear in front of all the guys, "Hey Eric, what's going on lately?"

I remember thinking, "That's a really odd question. This is not the time or place to just start a conversation or ask an open-ended question like that." Then I thought, "What's going on? What's going on! How in the world can I answer that? What sort of question is that? If he only knew what all was going on."

So, rather than try to give a rundown on everything, I just picked the Super Bowl experience that was just five days ago. I hadn't intended to tell the story, but frankly, it was the most recent spectacular or out-of-the-ordinary thing in a string of such occurrences, so I figured I might as well share that story.

As I wrapped up that story, a guy sitting to my left, Larry Landgren, asked, "Is that Jane Jones?"

I turned to him and, somewhat embarrassed, said, "I don't know. It was all so much, I never even asked the Merrits the name of their neighbor. I really have no idea what the name of this woman who has a brain tumor is or how I would really get in contact with her."

He replied, "Well, my wife has been tending to someone that sounds exactly like what you described–her name is Jane Jones and she is now at Southwest Christian Hospice."

When those words were spoken something in my soul just jumped back in shock. What are the chances that this is the same person, and that she is now at the same hospice that we had been at for six weeks leading up to Katie's passing?

Larry looked at me, and I looked at Chaplain Jim, and he looked back at us and we all had a similar bewildered but excited look. Simultaneously we all said, "I think we are supposed to go visit her ... today ... now."

And that is exactly what we did.

## I remember it like it was yesterday.

We each got in our car and followed one another for the half-hour drive to the hospice. I knew the drive well, as did Jim. On the way there, I took note of the weather – it was starting to snow. Snow had been forecast, and kids were told to stay home from school. Classes and events were being canceled.

But this did not deter us. In fact, the weather almost added to the somewhat out-of-body experience I was going through. You see, as I drove, I was reviewing all that had happened. When I woke up that day, I had no plan to go to the hospice and I had no idea who Jane Jones was. And yet, here I was, driving in the snow to a place that is both familiar and comfortable, but also foreboding and dreadful. But I am going nonetheless, following two of my spiritual brothers, on a mission to meet a stranger whom I had never met in response to a dream from another relative stranger from my church.

It was just kind of bizarre. Just what was I going to do or say when I got there? I wasn't sure, but a sense of calm started to settle over me as well. I knew that the Spirit would give me the words to say at the appropriate time, just as he had twice that week already. You see, scripture says also that we will often be called upon to give an account of our faith, to people of high stature and low. And, when we are asked to give an account or speak on behalf of the Lord, we should not worry about the words we will say, because it says that God, the Holy Spirit, will give us the words we need.

What a powerful commission and guarantee. We do not need to know in advance what we are to say – the words will be given to us. I was relying on that promise, and I had already seen it fulfilled twice that week – when I had opportunity to speak to Shirley, cancer patient number one; and Kassie, cancer patient number two. I will get to them in a while.

Then, another powerful thing hit me as I drove carefully through the snow toward the hospice. I was getting to see and probably speak with cancer patient number three, a woman named Jane whose name and whereabouts were unknown to me just minutes earlier. Now I was heading off in the snow, along with two of my close friends, to make contact with her.

Then it all came together with crystal clarity as I recalled my prayer from the previous Sunday night. I had prayed to the Lord that I would talk with these people, but I had also asked Him to make it happen – to open the necessary doors and get me in front of not one or two, but three different people.

**In less than a week, God had fully answered that prayer, orchestrating each of these meetings.**

The feeling that washed over me is hard to describe. It was energy and excitement, and anticipation all wrapped in one sensation. I felt on fire, even though I was walking into who knows what. It electrified me on the inside to know and to feel that God was indeed at work, and was in fact using me to do His work and His pleasure. I thought, "God is a multi-tasker and He makes it look easy."

It was scary as well – but in a good way. The way this all unfolded over the course of less than a week was almost mind-blowing. Stuff like this just didn't happen every day. I knew something big was happening, and I started to wonder if this was going to be some sort of new ministry for me – speaking to cancer patients and their families. I didn't feel a calling for this or feel that well prepared, but I knew that if God led me to this, He would lead me through this.

I asked, "What's wrong?"

At last one of them just looked me up and down and said, "You just can't imagine. We have cared for all sorts of patients here at Southwest Christian Hospice, but we have NEVER had one like Jane."

# Chapter Twenty-Seven: The nurses cried

Larry, Jim and I shook off the snow as we entered the hospice doors. To me, this place seemed almost like a transfer station – between this life and the next. It had a special sense of reverence about it.

Who knows how many souls left this earth from this spot and went on to the Kingdom of Heaven? Every time I parked in the parking lot, I glanced upward, almost expecting to see Jacob's ladder, or an escalator leading up into the sky with angels descending and ascending to escort souls into the Kingdom. I never saw anything like that, but it was easy to imagine it.

As we walked in, we were greeted with smiles and hugs by three hospice nurses that staffed the eight-room facility. They knew me and Jim from our repeated visits and meals spent there during the six weeks Katie spent under their marvelous care. After the words of greeting, they asked the obvious question, "Why are you visiting here?"

I almost didn't know where to start, but having told my story a number of times, I simply broke into an abridged version of my story, including the Merrits' Super Bowl party and his dream, and then about what had just happened at the Log House and how Larry had recognized the story and made the connection and – well – here we were.

There was this long, pregnant pause then two of these Hospice nurses started to cry.

I was taken aback. These were all pretty hardcore, veteran caregivers, each of whom had on average about 10 years serving in hospice care. They had seen all sorts of hard situations and helped countless people in their darkest days and helped encourage many family members as they faced and dealt with the passing of loved ones under their care. I had never seen any of them shed a tear or get too emotional. They were always pillars of quiet strength, ready to comfort others. I had never seen them in need of comfort.

I asked, "What's wrong?"

At last one of them just looked me up and down and said, "You just can't imagine. We have cared for all sorts of patients here at Southwest Christian Hospice, but we have NEVER had one like Jane."

I was speechless.

She went on. "You see, she is VERY ANGRY. So much so that we have to strap her down to her bed and often have to sedate her because if we don't she will attempt to roll off the bed and claw her way out of her room. You see, her brain tumor had caused her to become paralyzed on one side of her body and also unable to speak. So she had limited control of the other side and could roll out of the bed and attempt to make her way along the floor. Since she couldn't talk, she would show her anger by holding her breath till she turned blue."

These experienced nurses were saying that they had never quite encountered someone who was so angry and unwilling to accept their care and their cancer situation as this person Jane.

Finally, one nurse said, "We have been praying to the Lord to do something and, well, here you are."

At that point I was trying to process what they had just said. On one hand – what am I getting myself into? How am I going to be able to talk with or do any good with someone like that? This was quite different from what I was expecting. And finally, what did they mean "here you are?"

I thought, "Who am I? I am no one. I am not the person you think I am."

Then it hit me – they think I am an answer to their prayers.

It was a very unusual moment – to feel like nothing and yet be called an answer to prayer by three experienced hospice nurses who are apparently crying for joy and relief that I had just happened to show up.

Then it all became clear. I hadn't just happened to show up – this was a well-orchestrated plan of the Lord. An answer to my prayer as well, asking Him to make a way for me to get in front of each of these people. I knew that I had to go through that door and say whatever the Spirit gave to me to say.

I opened the door and met Jane.

Notice that, again, the Lord wouldn't send me on a mission alone. I had not one but two close friends and a back-up and three hospice nurses close by. Larry spoke to her first, introducing himself and describing who his wife was. He then introduced Jim who spoke. I don't remember what he said, but hey, he was a professional and knew all the appropriate things to say in a situation like this.

I was the amateur and I was thinking about just what in the world I was going to say. When it was my turn, all I could think to do was share what I had been sharing with others. I told her who I was and that my wife had been a patient in the same hospice a few weeks previously, and then I went into my dream.

Larry and Jim left.

I continued to share for about an hour. It was an unusual conversation because I did all the talking. Jane just lay there in bed with her eyes fastened upon me. I could tell from her facial expressions that she was patiently listening, rapidly taking in all I had to say. I really did not know what more to share.

At one point, when I was telling her all of this, I realized that she must be wondering what all this had to do with her. That's when a simple idea came to me and I shared it with her. I said to Jane, "Do you know what all this means? Obviously the Lord of Heaven is actively at work in all this. He is moving us around down here like pieces on a chess board. He was at work in the dream He gave to Brent, and the service of Larry's wife helping you, and the question that Russ asked, and the confirmation of my Log House brothers that led me, a complete stranger, to you, standing here right now at your bedside, just so I could share these powerful stories with you. This is God reaching out to you – telling you that He is the Lord of all things. He is the author of life and holds the keys of life and death."

My stories were being used to comfort Jane, literally on her deathbed. She was perhaps days away from passing away, and may not have even come to a place of saving grace. She certainly had no peace about her and was in great angst about what was happening. I said, "God has moved Heaven and earth to reach out to you, Jane. Please give your heart to Jesus Christ and put your trust in Him."

The entire time she listened very intently. Never once did I see the Jane that the others had described – a woman bound up in anger who held her breath to show her anger. She seemed to be calm and paying very close attention. I knew that God had gotten her attention.

Jane's eyes began to close. It was with effort she kept forcing her eyelids up. I also was getting tired and started to wonder about my drive home – the snow had continued to fall. The other thing on my mind was that this still seemed weird. I mean, I did not know this woman and here I was in her private room, in her deathbed room. I didn't even know her husband or really have any permission to be there. I had been told that he was a pilot for Delta and that he was off on a trip.

I started to get cold feet and was about to leave when she appeared to nod off. I decided that enough was enough and I did not want to say or do anything more until I had a chance to at least meet her husband. But as I was about to get up and leave I felt a prompting to just stay a little while longer and perhaps pray over her. So I did.

Midway of my prayer I heard a knock on the door. Assuming it was a nurse checking in on her, I did not immediately look up, but when I did, I saw a man standing in a uniform with a pilot's hat under his arm. Jane's husband. I thought, "What are the chances of that?"

I learned that his flight had been canceled due to the snow and that he had *just happened* to be able to stop in to see Jane. I explained my presence and what had led me to that point. About then, Jane seemed to wake up and we got her up and in a wheel-chair. After getting some ice cream to share, we pushed her down the hallway to a small chapel where I sat down and basically retold my story to her husband and added a few other details. This was

Jane's second hearing of my story – something that probably benefitted her as well.

It was a very encouraging visit – one I will remember all my life.

I drove home in the deep snow late that afternoon, confident that I had been used by God in a powerful way. A very rewarding tiredness swept over me – like how you feel after finishing some big project. I felt at one with the Spirit and had the rewarding sense of a job well done. It was truly an honor and a privilege to serve and be used by the Lord that way. I cannot describe the feeling any better. Once you experience it, you want to experience it again and again. Apart from my own personal dream vision experience, this encounter with Jane was and still is probably the next most spiritually impactful experience of my life. It is hard to describe the intense spiritual feeling that you receive when you are used by the Lord like that. It was simply fantastic.

I only visited Jane one other time. It was about a week or two later. The occasion was interesting as well. As I had reflected on all of these events and had had much conversation and counsel from others, they had all reinforced the idea that I probably ought to write a book about all of this. Everyone, except one person, fully affirmed this.

Another person pointed out that this surely must be a story that the Lord meant to be shared, because if it was only His purpose to give me and my family comfort and peace, the dream that I had would have been sufficient by itself. And I believe that is true – that one dose of God's grace would have been sufficient. But He went on and gave all these other people dreams and visions and then even this experience of reaching out to help bring one more lost sheep into His family and into His Country.

I suppose it was another prompting from the Spirit that I had this thought. I realized that if I were to write a book, I should record all of the testimonies of each person who had a dream or vision. And then it hit me that better than writing these down, I should get them recorded. So I found a videographer, Clark Hill, who did video recordings for Chick-fil-A events, and I asked him if he would professionally record each of us giving our version of events so it could be captured on video for future use. About a week or so after that encounter with Jane, I arranged for Clark to set up a camera in the parlor at SW Christian Hospice – it seemed like an appropriate location, and I was able to get all the people, with the exception of Amanda, the 10-year-old, because it was past her bedtime, to meet there one weeknight and record what we each had experienced from God. In just over an hour, we recorded our testimonies, one after the other, in one massive take. No editing or gaps.

It began with me telling my story. The camera was focused only on me as I set the stage and told what I experienced. Then the camera panned out and you could see on the video that I was surrounded by four others. I then took on the role of interviewer as I asked the others questions and they told what they experienced. It was a very powerful evening to hear each person, one after the other, share how God had touched their lives and shown them these deep mysteries. This was the first and only time each of these people had met each other or seen or heard the other people share their experiences in person, except Angela and Jackie who had been long-time friends and prayer partners. Chaplain Jim was also present when we filmed the testimonies as an off-camera witness.

When we wrapped up, we all filed down the corridor and went into Jane's room. We gathered around her and prayed for and prayed over her. It was a powerful time of prayer and the sense of the Holy Spirit was palpably in the room. It was a profoundly moving and rewarding moment. One that will echo in eternity.

I went on my own later that week and videotaped Amanda with her mother in their home, so I could also capture her testimony and have it inserted later during final editing.

It was then that it struck me that these stories were not simply small, isolated snippets or snapshots of spiritual truths. We recorded them in the order that they occurred and when you step back and look at them as a whole, they are all pieces of a larger mosaic.

**They each fit together to tell a much larger story. Together, they tell the Christian Story that all Believers are baptized into.**

We each will approach and go through our earthly death. When we do so, the Lord is keenly aware of our passing and is directly present – by our side when the grim reaper does his deed. And He is there to immediately administer the antidote, to give us the healing waters that will revive and refresh our spirits and our souls. We will be given a new life, an immortal life that cannot be taken away. We will be given a new body, one that is restored and renewed.

It will be all that God first imagined for us when He made us in His image and knitted us together in the womb. We will fulfill our destined design and purpose – to know and love and enjoy God forever. He will welcome us like a groom welcomes His bride, and will give us our first lavish birthday celebration when we are born into His kingdom and arrive for our welcome banquet in His Country. There will be laughing and rolling on the floor, and dancing – dancing and celebrating with the Lord in a beautiful setting – where the grass is greener and the breezes blow gently. The Lord has done the full work of the cross, ransoming our souls from death, having mastered and conquered the power of death, vanquishing it forever. He will not only restore us to our youth, but will heal us from all our infirmities as well as all our heartaches and wounds. We will have a new life and live it to the full.

That is what lies ahead for us. That is the greatest news of all time. Thanks be to God the Father, and His Son Jesus Christ, and to the Holy Spirit.

When angels appeared in her room, Katie knew she was about to be taken to Heaven and have a perfect, pain-free body. There is no way she could have been more excited. I got excited just hearing Jim Weathers tell about his conversation with Katie.

# Chapter Twenty-Eight: A Lost Sheep Is Rescued

After that incredible week ministering to others, I began to wonder if the Lord had other plans for my career than to continue to help sell chicken at Chick-fil-A. I was wondering if this was going to become some sort of new life calling or ministry. Although that week left me pretty worn out, I had to admit it was powerful and rewarding. But I really did not sense that I was supposed to transition to a new career field.

So I asked the Lord, "What was all of that?"

Eventually I got my answer. I don't remember exactly when I heard it or sensed it, but it became clear over time. The Spirit said to my spirit – these are examples for a chapter of the book.

I thought, "Oh, OK, what book?"

I had never written a book, and never seriously considered writing one. But now I had an unmistakable desire to get this story told – an act of obedience to the Lord, and as an act of love to help whomever the Lord intended to hear this story. Remember, we live in a divine partnership. God does His part, and we are supposed to do our part. I wanted to be sure I did my part and not let Him or anyone else down.

An irony is that I was known for writing excessively lengthy and detailed emails at work. I actually crashed the company server one weekend after a long email with lots of photos went out to the entire chain one Friday. It was such a large size that the entire network locked up. I thought I would be in big trouble the next week when word got around about my titanic-sized email and the crash. But it served a good purpose – after that the IT department did scans of emails and wouldn't let such a massive document go out on the network again.

I discovered the hard way that writing emails, even fairly long or epic emails, does not make you a writer. In fact, what I discovered in the weeks and years ahead was that, though I had a powerful story to tell, one that was simple and linear enough to me in my head, it was hard for me to get it all out on paper. After four or five major rounds of attempts to write the book, including a stint in a writers group, I was starting to get quite frustrated. I had lots of good starts, but things always seemed to get bogged down.

I felt torn between moving on with my life, but also living under this tremendous burden to get the book completed. It was quite frustrating. At one point, I almost gave up, thinking – who reads books today anyway? Perhaps I should just make the DVD available that I recorded initially.

But, remembering what the Lord has shown me – that I am supposed to not be anxious about anything but with prayer and petition with thankfulness I am to make my request of the Lord – I did. I said, "I am willing and eager to share the story You have entrusted to me – but I still need Your help."

I can't quite put into words what I sensed as a reply, but I just had this feeling that the Lord would send the right sort of help. I had no idea when or how or through whom, but I found a peace waiting again upon the Lord. Sometimes I worried that this may be some sort of cop-out – that if I really would focus I could do this myself. But I always got a sense to hold back and wait upon the Lord. Waiting on the Lord can be the hardest part.

Then earlier this year, the Spirit just seemed to plant some new ideas. First, I thought – what I really need is also an illustrator, because these dreams and scenes are really like vignettes – they ought to be visualized. Then I thought, since I am not sure anyone really reads books these days, perhaps a video or even a movie would be better. And then one day, out of the blue, God showed up again. Or at least, God seemed to prompt others in response to my prayer.

## Remember that guy Russ Breault?

He was the guy who asked from across the room, "Hey Eric, what's going on with you these days?" Well he did it again. Only this time, he asked, "Hey Eric, what are you doing next Wednesday morning? I am attending an event that I think you should attend with me."

Knowing that it is important to be interruptible and open to new things that may be a prompting from the Spirit, I asked about it and agreed to go. If my friend Russ invited me, this could be the Lord at work. You see, Russ is no ordinary guy. He is somewhat famous in faith circles. He is sometimes known as "the Shroud Guy' because for over two decades he has been fascinated about and become a teacher and presenter on one very specific subject – the Shroud of Turin. He has investigated it and the phenomena surrounding its possible creation for a long time. He may be the nation's leading authority on the subject and has appeared as an expert consultant on a number of TV shows, including some that have aired on the History Channel.

He also travels the country presenting his information on the subject and also witnessing and evangelizing for Christ in the process. You should look him up and perhaps see if you can attend one of his presentations near you. He does an outstanding job revealing the mysteries of this very unique article of history.

In any case, he also serves as an emcee of sorts for a local gathering on Wednesday mornings known simply as "the construction meeting." You see, this area of Georgia has recently become a big hub in the movie production industry, second only to Hollywood, California. One major studio is right in our back yard, so to speak. It is called Pinewood Studios and they recently opened a massive studio complete with eleven sound stages in the next town over. This is actually a venture that has had from its beginning a faith component. When the project first began, there was a weekly construction meeting held by the developer and their primary sub-contractors. It always ended in a time of prayer and sharing.

As the work on the studios drew to a close, the meeting just kept going. Over time it was opened up to the general public and word of mouth in the faith community had spread to the point that a large gathering of a hundred or more was common on any given week and brunch started to be served at the event. Now, there is a weekly lineup of speakers, both local and from beyond, that come in to share their testimonies.

It was to one of these events that Russ had felt prompted to invite me. There was a movie producer and director lined up to speak and Russ just thought I should hear his story and perhaps meet him and share mine with him afterward. So that is exactly what happened, I attended and heard a fantastic story of faith about how this director had started out and always kept a faith focus in his movie work.

At the end, Russ introduced me to him. We agreed to meet in the weeks ahead and I was excited to think – wow, perhaps we can skip the book and go straight to a movie.

Anyhow, we met over lunch, I shared the short version of my story and he and his wife both seemed to agree this was a story that needed to be told. Then he asked the important question – "So where is the book?"

I thought, "What book, aren't we going to just make a movie?"

And he made it clear to write the book. He said, "A movie like *Heaven is for Real* starts out as a book."

I knew this inside, but I was just getting caught up in the idea that someone else would be able to take this story and run with it, but it was becoming clear that a book was still a necessary foundation.

We will see if a movie is part of God's plan. I can see it, but then again, I can picture all of these stories in vivid detail and the impact of them is – well, more powerful than anything else I can imagine.

This is a spectacular reality – connecting the physical world we all live in and see and touch with the spiritual realm that we can only imagine and have only faith descriptions from a very few what the Kingdom of Heaven is really like. I mean, honestly, can there be any more important subject to explore?

So I was back at the need to write that book again. But this meeting that Russ had helped orchestrate that included a real movie producer and director was not for nothing – they helped introduce me to the idea of a ghostwriter. I thought, "Of course, someone to help me get this story told." I figured, when the going gets tough, sometimes it is time to call in a professional. Besides, perhaps this is how God would answer my prayer request – to send me someone to help so I would not be going it alone in this important mission.

And that is the story of how God continues to answer prayers and how this book finally came to be completed. His name is Jim Dobkins and I will let him share how he came to learn of this story and felt the prompting to help me bring this story to life and to you.

I contacted Wes Llewellyn in January 2017 as a result of seeing a post-Rapture film Wes and his wife Amanda had made years before. He showed interest in a Faith-Based property I have film rights to, but nothing blossomed from that. However, I let Wes know that my career path included ghostwriting books; also, that I was under conviction to move away from True Crime writing to major focus on Faith-Based properties.

Several weeks later I got an email from Wes:

"Do you still ghostwrite?"

I replied, "I'm available."

About two weeks later Wes introduced me to Eric via e-mail.

Eric and I started out in a ghostwriting relationship with him as sole author, and wound up as co-authors.

Whatever productive years I have left, I want to write books and scripts that truly help people. For me, this is a prayer-answer.

## So, what did He mean – a chapter for the book?

So, back to that answer from God that I sensed when I asked why he brought me into the lives of these three other families, each where the woman was passing from cancer. In some ways it was clear that I had helped Jane in particular, and I earnestly hoped and thought that my words were of some comfort and assistance to Kassie and Shirley.

But I still sensed there was more. Then it was the Spirit that seemed to make the link and confirm the need to write the book.

But, still, what was the connection with them and me or them and Katie's story?

When I thought about it, I did see some interesting truths emerge about each person's situation and how their stories played out, especially when comparing it to my wife Katie's story. On one hand, they each passed from their cancer, but how that played out seemed quite different in each case.

I think this is what God wanted me to reveal. They actually each illustrated four different postures or attitudes to hold as they lived and as they went on their own respective journeys through cancer and passage from this life.

Our story was simple and hard at the same time. But I can say that Katie maintained good spirits and a positive attitude throughout the five-year journey. On the other hand, Jane was tormented for almost her entire three-year journey that she fought cancer. These are two radically different experiences – one was filled with peace and serenity and the other with anger and angst. Which experience would you want?

Likewise, there were different levels of spiritual faith among these four women. On one end, there were two that had strong faith and they seemed to be quite calm and accepting of their situation. On the other hand, the other two seemed to have much less faith in the Lord, and had quite different reactions – one of anger and fear and the other, quite interestingly, had one of quiet academic detachment. Which posture would you want?

**My hope for – and advice to you – is to not wait until you are on your deathbed to ask Jesus into your life as personal Lord and Savior, if you are not yet a Believer. You never know how much time is left in your earthly life.**

I hate to get mathematical on anyone, but I think a chart would be helpful to explain what I have observed.

If we graph faith on one axis and peace on the other, and form four quadrants, you end up with four potential spaces.

Low Faith and Low Peace
Low Faith and High Peace
High Faith and Low Peace
High Faith and High Peace

Which posture would you want?

The answer suddenly seems clear – high faith and high peace.

I believe that each of these four women illustrated one of these four postures. I think it is very illuminating to take a look at this in a bit more detail.

The two extreme postures are pretty obvious:

High faith and high peace, like Katie had, which is what God wants Believers to have.

The very opposite – low faith and low peace, exemplified by Jane – is the place that so much of the world is in. If you have no faith in God and Heaven, then it is natural that there will be little peace at or about one's passing.

But the other two? What sort of position are they in? Let's look at each person's situation and response.

During the course of that week I was led to and able to meet with each of the three other women dealing with their late-stage cancer.

All three seemed in need of spiritual adjustments.

First, look closely at the chart on the next page. It has four quadrants, with 4 being the most desired quadrant.

Katie lived in the 4th quadrant. She had high faith and high peace. It made all the difference throughout her cancer journey.

The 4th quadrant is where God wants us to be, and where He wants us to strive for. He wants us to live life to the full, knowing our eternal life is secure in God's Country.

Katie was free of a lot of the pain, anger and angst that a lot of people might experience in her situation. She accepted and lived out her life with extraordinary peace and grace. She ministered to many others, spreading God's message of grace and peace even while in hospice.

Truly, Katie lived like Paul at the end of her days. Every day she lived she could live as Christ. And when she would graduate to Heaven, she knew it would be gain. She was at total peace with that.

## Faith Chart

### Four Quadrants

| | | |
|---|---|---|
| **High Faith** | 3. <u>Kassie</u><br>Spiritually striving, clinging and demanding, fighting "evil" | 4. <u>Katie</u><br>Spiritually serene, deep-rooted faith, surrendered |
| **Low Faith** | 1. <u>Jane</u><br>Spiritually uncertain, personally filled with anger and unrest | 2. <u>Shirley</u><br>Spiritually asleep, "clinical" view of her own death |
| | Low Peace | High Peace |

When angels appeared in her room, Katie knew she was about to be taken to Heaven and have a perfect, pain-free body. There is no way she could have been more excited. I got excited just hearing Jim Weathers tell about his conversation with Katie.

One of the other three ladies – Kassie – was a devoted Christian. Shirley might have been a Christian, but I do not know for sure. All three ladies had attitude issues. I will discuss Shirley and Kassie first, and then Jane, a person full of anger and unrest. She was the lost sheep God wanted to rescue.

## Shirley

This is one of the quadrants that may seem hard to understand for some, but may be easy for others to imagine. This is the low faith or perhaps no faith individual who actually is at a high level of peace about their passing. A scientist and educator, Shirley had pancreatic cancer. She had low faith but a high peace outlook. Her husband was also an academic, a high school engineering teacher.

Both had a very cool, clinical view about death.

Shirley was matter-of-fact about her pending death. She expressed no angst, and showed no indication of hope or excitement about Heaven. When I broached the subject in my only meeting with her, she said, "People live and people die. Some people get cancer and some will die from cancer. I will be one of those people."

And that was that. There was no emotion, no additional thoughts, no mention of God or faith whatsoever. I was so stunned, I did not know what to say. I went in prepared to have a long discussion about God and faith, and instead, I seemed to get nothing. Almost a dead spiritual pulse.

I really don't know the spiritual posture or position of faith of Shirley I did not know her or know their family well. They held no church or memorial service at her death; instead holding a graveside event at a cemetery in another state, attended by family only. Only God knows the true condition of a person's heart and where they stand with Him and their faith. Only God knows who is and is not in the Kingdom of Heaven. I am not prepared to make a definitive statement on whether Shirley was saved. I can only speculate based on what I observed. Hopefully, she was a person of quiet and strong faith, not comfortable in sharing with a stranger, even if it was someone like me who she did know who I was and that my wife had recently passed from cancer and that both our 10-year-old daughters were friends and going through this loss experience together. I will make no judgment about her – only that I hope to see her in God's Country.

I am just pointing out the cold, detached image she projected about the subject of her own death. It would seem in keeping with an atheist or someone who had little if any Judeo-Christian set of beliefs. My point is not to say anything negative, just to point out the quadrant in the chart that Shirley seems to represent. It is a quadrant people can be in and she seemed to be in it.

I did not feel any additional prompting to share anything more with her – though I was there for that purpose and eager to do so. The spirit seemed to go silent at that visit. I don't know what else to say. I pray she had some sort of quiet and very personal faith, but only God knows.

## Kassie

When I first learned of Kassie's first round of cancer, she was the one who described it as a "touch of breast cancer" at a Relay for Life event. She'd been the receptionist at a corporation's home office, a friendly face I saw at times.

Kassie was a quiet, sweet person of deep, abiding faith. She and her husband had what anyone would have to describe as a very strong faith. I may go out on a limb here to describe that they were members within a very unique camp within the Christian community. Based on my experience visiting with them and hearing from others who attended the same church, I became aware of the somewhat specific set of beliefs that the church seemed to teach and project. They were taught and were strong believers in the power of prayer for complete healing. They downplayed and opted out of a lot of traditional medicine's approaches to cancer and other diseases as well. Instead, they focused on prayer and homeopathic remedies.

One view that is somewhat common in this *camp* is that Believers should be able to pray for and receive healing for all types of illness, but taken to an extreme, this concept can be taken so far as to say that, if a person is not being healed, then perhaps there is something wrong spiritually. This could mean that not everyone is praying in agreement or that the person involved has some spiritual stronghold of evil that is working this disease process, preventing the healing power of God from fully working.

To me, this seems as if it sort of sets up a power struggle between God and the powers of darkness. And it can set up an idea that somehow the faith of the person is somehow lacking, just not good enough, or that other people around them are just not praying hard enough.

You may be able to see that this kind of thinking can set up a pretty horrible situation. It is a contradictory posture of believing in the power of prayer, but also believing that it is based on the works of the Believer or the people praying, or that God's power is not sovereign enough to act in all cases. This can put a whole lot of pressure on people in this camp – they had better get well and be healed of their diseases or it may essentially reveal the sin in their lives or that they just are not living right.

This is actually the foundation of the concept of the Christian work ethic. In Puritan days, there was a form of a prosperity gospel that took the shape of the following belief system. The idea was that if you were living right before God He would prosper you by granting you favor and wealth. The situation this set up was that people wanted to be right with God and wanted to appear to be right with God, so it was noted that this branch of Protestants seemed to be really hard workers.

## Do you get the picture?

They all collectively started to be very industrious. Not that that is a bad thing to be hard working and not lazy, but it is the reason behind it.

Are you doing it to simply excel and reap the benefits of your effort?

Or is this a kind of works-based faith?

Or is it also a kind of program where in order to appear to be righteous, you want to be successful and appear to be receiving the blessings of God?

Well, one way to be successful in the eyes of the world is actually the result of just good old-fashioned hard work. So while some may in fact be walking closely with God, as a group they gained the reputation of successful hard workers – hence the

Protestant work ethic. But this does not have anything to do with their standing with God.

I am not saying there is anything wrong with hard work. But if you believe that your hard work makes you acceptable to God – and is your ticket to get into Heaven – then please read again Chapter Twenty-One where we talk about the work of faith. It is simply to confess with your mouth and believe in your heart that Jesus Christ is Lord.

That is it.

Worldly success is unnecessary. Scripture has lots of warnings about money, wealth, storing up for yourself treasure on earth vs. treasure in Heaven.

I believe this *camp* may be misguided in this area as it concerns prayers to God. It seems to smack of a works-based prayer model. This is not how it works. God says that the prayers of others can be sufficient. He demonstrates that a distant prayer from a centurion is sufficient to heal a servant. He shows how the prayers of friends who lower a man down through a hole in the roof are sufficient. He shows how faith of a woman who merely touches His robe is sufficient for healing. It says faith as small as a mustard seed is sufficient to move a mountain into the sea. So, where is the idea that the quality or quantity of faith of the prayers of those being prayed for is insufficient?

Finally, there is a concept that I touched on earlier that I feel I should reiterate here. It is the idea that God does and can heal, but sometimes there are other factors going on that we know not of. And there is a concept that I understand this way. When we pray for healing, and I usually am praying for healing of people in their body to return to this life with a level of health; I also believe we need to be open to and prepared that the Lord may heal the person in Heaven.

If we have a true understanding and faith in the Kingdom of Heaven, this should be easier to accept and understand. For when that happens you are healed in the highest way possible – you have been healed in a way that death and disease can no longer touch or impact. You have been freed totally from this body that is subject to death. Scripture describes that and also that we will be raised incorruptible. In other words, raised in a way that we can no longer be susceptible to injury or death.

Could any healing be more complete than that?

## So, back to Kassie.

She and her husband were in that camp within Christianity and would have to be categorized in the high faith category, but I would also have to put them in the low peace corner of the chart because I sensed they were not at peace on the inside.

On the outside they kept up a strong spiritual appearance and outlook. But I think on the inside they were devastated that their approach in faith that God would provide a full healing based on the proper prayer of a righteous person availing much did not work out like they expected. There was a pulling away from people that did not pray exactly like them. I could see a degree of isolation and utter frustration when it became more and more obvious that the cancer was not being cured or healed.

When I shared my story that evening over dinner in their home, they seemed to listen quietly, patiently and respectfully, but I never felt the full embrace of their conversation. It was like I was stepping into their *camp* but I was not wearing their uniform and wasn't saying the sorts of things that they would be expecting to hear.

I ended up hearing some more from another friend and colleague who was a member of their particular church. When his wife passed from cancer, he confirmed the prevailing belief I am talking about here. In fact, his daughter said some really powerful and moving things at the memorial service for her mother – things that I know and others confirmed were not in full agreement with the prevailing beliefs of that church. It must be hard to be in that *camp*. I pray God opens the eyes and provides a more merciful interpretation to those in that *camp*. God is a god of great mercy and kindness. He does not desire sacrifice – Jesus was the sacrifice and satisfied it once and for all – we no longer live under the old covenant where previously the Lord did require a sacrifice. What

God does require is simply a contrite and humble heart. Merely believe in your heart and confess with your mouth and you will be saved. It is that simple and that easy. According to Psalm 116:15, "Precious in the sight of the LORD is the death of His faithful servants."

They assumed and almost seemed to demand answered prayer in the form of full healing from the start. When it didn't work out that way, it was a big blow to that model of faith. In their case, I do believe that eventually their strong faith got them closer into a place of peace at the end, but I sensed a lot of striving in a spiritual way. I attended the memorial service for Kassie, and I sensed that there was peace and faith in the end.

I believe that Kassie was healed in the highest form of healing and was welcomed with a banquet into God's Country in the same way that we saw Katie get welcomed. But many people just can't accept that answer or outcome. Thus, it robs them of peace even if they have strong faith.

## Jane

A true lost sheep, she was angry at God from the first onset of her cancer, and full of unrest about everything. She was beyond listening to reason for most of the three years since the Big C diagnosis.

Nurses could not make headway with her.

Nor anyone else.

It was and is understandable. Anger is often one of the first emotions I experience as well when I am disappointed. God is working on that with me – we are to be slow to anger and quick to bless. But I can understand fully how much of a shock and disappointment it would be to suddenly have the happy trajectory of our lives sent spiraling down, out of control – like a plane with an engine on fire, spinning out of control toward the ground. This is not how the trip was supposed to be – we all plan for and hope for our happy little life.

Cancer is like a roaring dragon that seems immensely threatening from the onset. And if you were to become suddenly paralyzed, when you are in the prime of your life with your health and your family all going well, it would be a shock and a mighty disappointment. I can totally relate to being angry. It always amazed me that Katie did not ever go down that path. I know I would have.

In Jane's case, her cancer brought on paralysis on one side of her body and took her power of speech. That is a pretty harsh turn of events for anyone. So, after three years of Jane being essentially trapped inside her own body, and her husband and fellow members of the community all doing their best to care for her, something very interesting and powerful happened. Her husband broke down and prayed and things began to change, even in the final days and weeks of her life.

Her husband was a pilot and did have the support of many in the community to help him care for his wife. But one fateful night, he had reached the end of his ability to cope and described how he had broken down and cried out to God on the floor of his living room. The collective toll of caring for his wife, and her constant anger and deteriorating symptoms, had taken their toll. He needed help and had nowhere else to turn.

He asked for help and had been praying throughout their entire cancer journey for two things – that she would have peace and salvation.

When he cried out, he described to me that he simply felt God's reassuring presence surround him as he prayed on the floor. The next day, in what seemed almost like a coincidental conversation that he just happened to overhear from two strangers, he learned about SW Christian Hospice. When he dialed the number and explained his situation, they first said that their eight-bed facility was full. But after taking another look at their records, the receptionist said, "A space just opened up. If you could come in, we probably can help you."

Jane was admitted the next day.

God had moved things in Heaven and on earth to reach out to this one lost sheep, and though she was not even able to speak, I believe that she made a death-bed confession of faith in Jesus, moving from the first to the fourth quadrant. In fact, I have this on pretty good authority that both of her husband's prayers were finally and fully answered.

You see, Jane continued on for another couple weeks after I had my encounter with her and then her husband on that fateful Friday, just five days after the final dream vision that Brent Merritt had received. I attended the funeral and wanted to stay in contact with her husband. It was a few weeks after her passing that I finally had an opportunity to get together with her husband, Frank, and just talk, man-to-man, as two people can talk who have both been through a similar ordeal or hardship. He came over to my house and we talked for hours, sharing stories from our journeys.

When it was very late, I walked him out to his car. As he was opening the car door, he paused and turned to me and said something very impactful that will stay with me the rest of my life:

"Over and over I prayed just two simple prayers for Jane – her salvation, and that she would calm down and have peace. I believe that both of my prayers were answered."

He told me that until I visited, she was continually angry and unable to accept what she thought God had done to her. She could not accept that she was not going to live out the life she had planned on this earth. But, somehow, he said that that all changed after my visit. After that she was no longer angry, but accepted the Lord and passed in peace.

She's in God's Country.

No more partial-body paralysis from the cancer.

A new, youthful, perfect body.


One last footnote. When Jane's husband told me about the day he called the hospice in desperation, and how the person answering first said the facility was full, but checked again and said there was an opening, he happened to mention the date. It's funny, I had not asked him the date or the timeline, but he said it anyway.

I was stunned silent for a moment. Brent Merritt's Super Bowl Sunday dream in which Katie told him to have me talk to his neighbor's wife, suddenly became even more meaningful.

The day he called the hospice, and the day that one room became available was on January 14, 2010.

The day Katie passed into God's Country.

Just another coincidence?

## Powerful scene from a great movie

I love great movies, especially those that help illustrate some powerful eternal truth. Such movies include The Matrix, The Legend of Bagger Vance, Braveheart, and the Kingdom of Heaven. Another such movie is Gladiator. There is a powerful scene at the very end of that movie that draws its power because it retells the most powerful story ever told – God's story.

It illustrates death and resurrection and restoration and, because we are His children, it is our story as well. The scene I am referring to is the final scene where the main character, the Gladiator, played by Russel Crow, kills the evil emperor Commodus. But while doing so, he has suffered a mortal wound in the battle. His life and this final battle serve to also signify our lives and the struggles and hardships we all endure throughout our earthly life. Like it says in scripture – in this world you will have troubles. But we are to take heart for God has overcome the world.

In the final climax of the movie, as the gladiator shares his final words, the queen leans over him and, realizing he is dying, tells him to "go to them," meaning that he should feel released to die in peace and go to his family that is awaiting him in heaven. The movie flashes in a vision showing his wife and family, who earlier in the story had been savagely killed but now are shown to be restored alive and well, running to the gladiator, as he comes home, also restored, in an idyllic field of golden wheat. This is what the movie calls Elysium or heaven. As his body dies, the movie screen seems to show his body being lifted up and transported to a heavenly place as the camera pans up to the heavens.

And the filmmaker even squeezes in one last little scene within the scene – it shows a friend and fellow gladiator who walked alongside the gladiator for much of the story and who also survived the battle but is still alive on earth. He is thinking of and missing his friend and is honoring his fallen comrade by burying some little statues that the Gladiator had used to pray over concerning his family. The friend buries these statues and says, confidently and almost defiantly, "I WILL see you again … just not yet, not yet."

That is our story. We WILL see our loved ones and all who have gone on ahead of us again. Just not yet, not yet.

Two quotes from C.S. Lewis's book, *The Last battle*, paint a glorious picture of God's Country:

"I have come home at last! This is my real country! I belong here. This is the land I have been looking for all my life, though I never knew it till now...Come further up, come further in!"

"And as He spoke, He no longer looked to them like a lion; but the things that began to happen after that were so great and beautiful that I cannot write them. And for us this the end of all the stories, and we can most truly say that they all lived happily ever after. But for them it was only the beginning of the real story. All their life in this world and all their adventures in Narnia had only been the cover and the title page: now at last they were beginning Chapter One of the Great Story which no one on earth has read: which goes on forever: in which every chapter is better than the one before."

I love that marvelous picture and how Lewis compares all that we know now and all our adventures in this life as but the cover and title page of God's book of our lives with Him that goes on and on and never ends. It takes my breath away to imagine that this is what our Lord has planned for us.

## Epilogue: Clara's Confirmation

As I said earlier in the book and I shared with my children, we were not going to hold back and stop living. In fact, if anything, we had a renewed sense and assurance of God's providence and protection.

I knew that I would never again feel alone or that I was to go it alone. God was always with me and would never abandon or forsake me. Also, God had a well-established track record of sending someone to help me, to be with me, so that I was not going to go it alone.

It wasn't that long when I wondered, "Lord, what do you have next for me, or whom do you have next for me?" I loved my wife and would miss her, but she had also released me in that touching conversation in her final weeks of life.

The time came when I felt led to venture out and see whom the Lord would lead me to or bring to me. I knew this could take a while and I was prepared for it to take a long time. I knew that I would need to be careful, and always prayerful.

Having been out of the dating world for 25 years, I figured I'd better be willing to learn a new approach and try the online dating process. I chose to try Chemistry.com. Unlike most dating sites that allow you to choose your faith profile and perhaps the desired faith profile you may have for any potential matches, this site also let you complete an optional statement of faith. I liked that feature very much.

I filled out the optional statement of faith in length, believing that would be the best way to sift through potential matches as well as to let others know in no uncertain terms where I was in my faith journey.

At this point in my life, I really needed someone who was deep enough in her faith to be able to walk side by side with me – the term you sometimes hear is equally yoked – someone that is close to where you are in your own faith journey. It would take someone of deep faith and understanding to hear my story and be able to relate to me on all these subjects.

Using a site that allowed for a faith statement turned out to be a smart approach because it eliminated most people simply because they didn't bother or didn't have enough conviction about their faith to fill out that section. It made my search much easier. I only read profiles where the person could at least give a sound and sincere statement of her faith. Because this is the most fundamental need for agreement in any romantic relationship or marriage. You really need to be on equal foundation for your relationship to flourish.

After a few months and some screening interview dates, I went on the most amazing date of all – a woman who listened to my story and understood the deep matters of faith.

Clara also had two children – Matthew and Christina. A rather interesting coincidence as my two children are Matthew and Kristen.

We hit it off, and quickly were comfortable with each other. We shared a deep, personal, abiding faith in Christ.

Over time and much prayer it became clear that the Lord had brought us together for this unique season of our lives. We both sensed that level of being equally yoked. Thought she had quite a different background from my own, she had arrived at essentially the same solid ground of faith, but by a completely different set of life experiences.

Clearly the Lord had arranged all of this. And His timing and the ease of it all made Him again seem like a multi-tasker and that He made it all look easy. Doesn't it say in scripture that "the Lord is not slow as some consider slowness?"

I felt that the Lord was willing and able to move quickly to bring to me another wife, what the Bible calls an ezer kenegdo – a term that is only used twice in all of scripture. It means a trusted and intimate helpmate. The only other time it is used is when God refers to Himself as a trusted helpmate to His children. This is what Clara is for me. She is a quiet person of deep and profound faith, whom God has seen fit to bless me with.

## One last story

A most interesting thing happened that I did not find out about until later, after Clara and I were engaged to get married:

While we were dating, Clara was praying. Unlike me, she has been praying and walking intimately with God for a long time, since she was a little girl. And praying and asking to hear from God was not a new thing for her, as it was for me. In a prayer one day, Clara was pondering a future with me and she made a request to God for a specific sign – on a specific day – to confirm that I was truly the person the Lord was leading her to.

She had always had a close, intimate prayer life, and was never shy about asking for a sign.

We were driving to pick up my kids from relatives who'd watched them for a few days. Along the way – unbeknownst to me – she asked the Lord for a confirming sign: She had asked that she would see a butterfly on that particular day.

Later when she told me this story I was surprised, mainly as we were driving on an Interstate all day, and she was sleeping most of the trip. If you were asking the Lord for a sign to see a butterfly, it would seem difficult to see that while driving down the highway at 75 miles an hour or while sleeping.

We'd agreed to meet my relatives at a restaurant. When we got there, my daughter Kristen ran to give Clara and me hugs.

She was wearing a shirt that had a big butterfly on it.

P.S. – Clara and I married on July 31, 2011. Jamie Bosworth was my best man.

### Publisher's Note

**To arrange book signings and media interviews with Eric Stogner, direct your request to publisher@ucspress.com. Visit www.intogodscountry.com for updated news about this book and Eric's public appearances.**

CPSIA information can be obtained
at www.ICGtesting.com
Printed in the USA
FFOW01n2155160418
46253282-47656FF

9 780943 247205